P9-CCW-814

Fasting has become one of the most important elements of my faith in recent years. If you are feeling spiritually dull, *The Fasting Edge* will sharpen your focus and empower you to serve Christ with your whole heart.

—CRAIG GROESCHEL
PASTOR OF LIFECHURCH.TV
AUTHOR, *WEIRD BECAUSE NORMAL ISN'T WORKING*

Some of the most pivotal times in my entire life have come during or after seasons of fasting. It's impossible to overstate its potential to propel you to a whole new level in your walk with Christ and unlock potential you never knew you had. And it's almost equally impossible to overstate Jentezen's ability to equip you to do it. *The Fasting Edge* is essential reading for anyone wanting to leave spiritual mediocrity behind and embrace the kind of life God always intended you to have.

—STEVEN FURTICK
LEAD PASTOR, ELEVATION CHURCH
AND AUTHOR, *SUN STAND STILL*

The fasting EDGE

Jentezen Franklin

CHARISMA
HOUSE

Most CHARISMA HOUSE BOOK GROUP products are available at special quantity discounts for bulk purchase for sales promotions, premiums, fund-raising, and educational needs. For details, write Charisma House Book Group, 600 Rinehart Road, Lake Mary, Florida 32746, or telephone (407) 333-0600.

THE FASTING EDGE by Jentezen Franklin
Published by Charisma House
Charisma Media/Charisma House Book Group
600 Rinehart Road
Lake Mary, Florida 32746
www.charismahouse.com

Unless otherwise noted, all Scripture quotations are from the New King James Version of the Bible. Copyright © 1979, 1980, 1982 by Thomas Nelson, Inc., publishers. Used by permission.

Scripture quotations marked AMP are from the Amplified Bible. Old Testament copyright © 1965, 1987 by the Zondervan Corporation. The Amplified New Testament copyright © 1954, 1958, 1987 by the Lockman Foundation. Used by permission.

Scripture quotations marked NIV are from the Holy Bible, New International Version. Copyright © 1973, 1978, 1984, International Bible Society. Used by permission.

Some names of persons mentioned in this book have been changed to protect privacy; any similarity between individuals described in this book to individuals known to readers is purely coincidental.

Visit the author's website at www.jentezenfranklin.org.

Library of Congress Cataloging-in-Publication Data

Franklin, Jentezen, 1962-
  The fasting edge / Jentezen Franklin.
      p. cm.
  Includes bibliographical references (p.   ).
  ISBN 978-1-61638-584-2 (casebound) -- ISBN 978-1-61638-
629-0 (e-book) -- ISBN 978-1-61638-625-2 (international trade
pbk.) 1. Fasting--Religious aspects--Christianity. I. Title.
  BV5055.F732 2011
  204'.47--dc23
                                    2011031723

This publication is translated in Spanish under the title *El ayuno de vanguardia*, copyright © 2011 by Jentezen Franklin, published by Casa Creación, a Charisma Media company. All rights reserved.

11 12 13 14 15 — 9 8 7 6 5 4 3 2
Printed in the United States of America

*Lovingly dedicated to my brother,
Richie, whose ministry I was saved
under, who gave me my first
opportunity to preach, and who taught
me so much about the power of fasting.*

Acknowledgments

A special thank-you to my wife, Cherise, who constantly inspires me, and to our children Courteney, Caressa, Caroline, Connar, and Drake, who are a blessing to me each and every day.

Steve Strang, Tessie DeVore, and the Charisma House team—thank you for partnering with me to publish this book and for always going the extra mile for excellence.

Tomi Kaiser, your gift has enabled me to reach many through print. You are the engine behind this book and my favorite to work with.

To all the incredible Free Chapel staff—thank you for your dedication to this ministry.

To the greatest executive team: Tracy Page, Natasha Phillips, Brian Smith, and Caressa Franklin—thank you for all you do to ensure this ministry's success.

Lastly, thank you to the Free Chapel congregation and Kingdom Connection partners for your support as we continue spreading the gospel locally and globally.

Contents

Introduction

I t happens to all of us. We keep going and going, and before we realize it, we just don't seem to be as effective at anything as we used to be. Has your passion for the Lord waned from when you were first born again? Does it feel as if you have lost steam since the last conference or revival meeting you attended? Has "life" begun to wear you down to the point that serving the Lord has become just one more appointment to keep on the weekly calendar, falling somewhere between work, meals, and getting the kids to practice? Have you grown weary of the same old routine at work? Do you find yourself flaring up in your relationships with family and friends more readily? More to the point, have you simply grown *dull*?

Abraham Lincoln is known for making the statement, "Give me six hours to chop down a tree, and I will spend the first four sharpening the ax." For many of us that sounds like a waste of at least three and a half of those six hours. But remember, Lincoln was a skilled woodsman, having cut down trees, chopped firewood, and split rails to build fences since his youth. His experience even became part of his campaign slogan when his party dubbed him "the Rail Candidate" in this country's 1860 presidential elections, a reference to his common-man rail-splitting days. Two facts Lincoln knew very well, as do all who work with such tools:

1. A dull ax makes for far more work
2. A dull ax can be much more dangerous than a well-sharpened one.

Using a dull ax requires more physical effort and time to cut down the same number of trees as using a well-sharpened one. Since a dull ax will not bite into the wood, one powerful swing can result in it glancing off of the intended target and cutting into one's leg instead. Years of experience made Lincoln keenly aware that the right tools properly cared for make hard work more successful. He may have even read Solomon's wise counsel on the subject in Ecclesiastes 10:10:

> If the ax is dull,
> And one does not sharpen the edge,
> Then he must use more strength;
> But wisdom brings success.

"Wisdom" is taking the required time to sit down with a file, an ax stone, and some oil to put the proper edge back on the ax. With the file you slowly grind away the larger imperfections and burrs. Using a fine stone in a circular motion further hones the edge and removes the remaining shiny spots that indicate the blade is still dull. Rubbing a small amount of oil along the edge helps to remove the bits of shavings and debris that have been ground down. It is a process, and anyone familiar with the process will tell you that a power grinder is never to be used to speed things up. Hastening the process that way actually softens the steel in the ax head, leaving it completely useless.

Every believer loses the edge in his or her life from time to time. Trudging on in our own strength through our daily routines can make us increasingly dull, ineffective, and even dangerous. Individuals, ministries, and entire churches can lose the edge.

You regain the edge in your life in much the same way that you regain the edge on an ax—by stopping what you are doing and carefully applying the right tools. Declaring a spiritual fast is a means of interrupting the dulling effects of life's routines. Fasting is taking time to regain the edge, preparing the way for you to accomplish so much more though the power of the Holy Spirit than you could accomplish through your own limited strength. Fasting, prayer, and time reading God's Word work together just like the woodsman's tools used to sharpen an ax. When I fast privately or corporately, it allows me to regain the cutting edge of the anointing and Holy Spirit in my life.

In my first book, titled *Fasting*,[1] I posed the question that if Jesus could have done what He was sent to do on this earth without fasting, why did He fast? Immediately following His baptism, the Bible tells us that the Holy

Spirit led Jesus into the desert on a forty-day fast. If the Son of God fasted, and He is our example, I cannot say often enough how crucial the discipline of fasting and prayer must be to the Christian life.

On one of my first trips to Israel I had the opportunity to record a message while standing in front of a vast stretch of wilderness to those who partner with our ministry. Though I was at that location for only a little while, I thought about how brutal the conditions in that land must have been. It is a place of extremes, very dry and hot during the day but cold at night. Most of us want our walk with God to be mild and comfortable. Be careful: the alternative to the extremes is lukewarm, and Jesus is not a fan of lukewarm.[2] But there is a place of power and anointing that we can never experience without being led into the wilderness, coming away from everyone and everything else to seek God in fasting and prayer. After all, that was the first thing Jesus did after the Father announced to the world, "This is My beloved Son, in whom I am well pleased" (Matt. 3:17). Jesus stood up from the baptismal waters of the Jordan River and was led by the Holy Spirit into the wilderness where He fasted for forty days and nights.

Someone may say, "My *life* is a wilderness! It's barren. It's empty. It's dry." If this describes your life, your marriage, your hopes and dreams—it is time to fast and pray. Perhaps the Holy Spirit has led you to this place to regain your edge. I want to encourage you that it is time to stop striving in your own strength and press in to see what He has for you in the wilderness. Jesus fasted and was victorious over the temptations of the devil at the end of that grueling wilderness fast. Luke tells us that after the fast, "Jesus returned in the power of the Spirit to Galilee, and news of Him went out through all the surrounding region" (Luke 4:14).

Like sharpening an ax, fasting is a short season that produces a lasting effect. Out of 365 days in a year, 21 days is not that long to take a break from your routine and experience a fresh encounter with God. We fast corporately as a church at the beginning of every year because that short season sets the course for the rest of the year. By March or April I no longer remember the difficulty of that long 21-day fast in January. But God does not forget. His promise in Hebrews 11:6 is true: "Without faith it is impossible to please Him, for he who comes to God must believe that He is, and that He is a rewarder of those who diligently seek Him."

We need the cutting edge back. We need the cutting edge back in our prayer life. Leaders, pastors, teachers...we need the cutting edge back in our preaching and ministry. We need the cutting edge back in our churches. We need the cutting edge back in our finances. People frequently ask me how Free Chapel continues to grow and how our campuses are debt free. I can only point to the faithfulness of the Lord. We honor Him with the firstfruits. For the last twelve years we have set out to seek Him diligently at the beginning of each year in a corporate fast and throughout the year with individual fasts as people feel led to do so. He is a rewarder! Over the years we have seen miraculous testimonies of God's healing power, mended marriages, and deliverance from devastating addictions of all kinds in individual lives (many of these stories are highlighted in *Fasting*). Our people have seen financial breakthroughs like never before.

But God's blessings always overflow the cup. We must never stay focused on our own needs so much that we neglect the needs of others. When you make fasting part of your lifestyle, you begin to hear His heart to release the captives and meet the needs beyond your own borders in ever increasing measure. At the writing of this book, we have been able to sow millions of dollars into Mission: Bread of Life and Life Speakers, two ministries we have launched to help feed the hungry, provide medical aid, build homes for those left devastated by natural disasters, and assist in building rehabilitation centers for those rescued from human trafficking.

The world needs a people of God who walk in the anointing and power of the Holy Spirit that pulls down strongholds and sets the captives free! But there are no "people of God" without there first being a willing "person of God." If you are tired of dull church, if you are tired of a cold, dry, barren relationship with Jesus, it is time to regain the edge. It is time to declare a spiritual fast. The Bible declares that "the steps of a good man are ordered by the LORD, and He delights in his way" (Ps. 37:23). I believe God is going to establish who He is in your life again, afresh and anew. The victory that Jesus won against the devil when He fasted forty days established a pattern for you and me to follow. Perhaps you have fasted and have seen God bless you and do mighty things in your life. Remember, fasting gets you in a position to receive personal blessing and guidance for your life, and also for God to use you to reach others with His power. It is time to regain the edge so we can do far more by the Spirit of God than we could ever accomplish with our own strength.

Chapter 1

You Need to Regain the Edge

The question "What does fasting do?" is one I have been asked more times than I can remember. My answer is always the same: Fasting and prayer bring you closer to God. While that may be a brief answer, it is by no means simplistic.

Fasting is not a requirement. Fasting is a *choice*. Whenever a believer chooses to begin a spiritual fast for one day or for several days, he or she makes a choice to break out of the routine in order to draw closer to God. I chose to develop a lifestyle of prayer and fasting over twenty-five years ago, and I do not know of anything that has been more powerful in my Christian life. It is true in my personal experience and it is true for our church, as evidenced by the multitude of powerful testimonies that stem from our annual corporate fast at Free Chapel. I am more convinced than ever that fasting is a gateway through which God releases His supernatural power into our lives. The choice is ours: we can either open that gateway or ignore it and keep on going in our routines.

For the past twelve years our church has committed to an annual twenty-one-day fast in January. With each passing year I become more certain that this annual fast, set aside to honor God with the "first" of our year, is truly part of His design and calling. I have witnessed profound miracles in this church and through this ministry as we have determined to seek God in fasting and prayer, things that could not have come about in our own strength or effort. I was amazed to discover that nearly a million people visited our fasting website[1] during a two-day period on our recent annual fast. People all over America and the far reaches of the world are beginning to see that fasting is not just for a select few—but that God *is* a rewarder of all who *diligently* seek Him.[2]

> Fasting and prayer bring you closer to God. While that may be a brief answer, it is by no means simplistic.

Fasting is a short season that releases long-term rewards. It is like taking the time to sharpen your ax before cutting down a tree. As with most lumberjack lore, one tale has circulated for years about two lumberjacks having a tree-cutting competition. In his book *Tony Evans Speaks Out on Fasting*, Dr. Evans references a version of this amusing story to illustrate a key point related to fasting.[3] As the story goes, a strong, young lumberjack challenged a respected veteran lumberjack to a contest. The young man wanted to prove himself, believing that he could cut more trees in one day than the older man. The contest began early one morning. Relying on his own strength and stamina, the young man began swinging his ax through first one tree and then another. As the day progressed, he was certain he was winning because he could see that the old man was taking several breaks. All the while the young man just kept swinging his ax, felling one tree after another. At day's end, the young man stood confidently by, waiting for the official count from the other lumberjacks. To his shock and dismay, the old lumberjack had cut down at least a third more trees than the younger man. In frustration the young lumberjack conceded victory to his veteran competitor, but he wanted to know the man's secret. He wanted to know how he managed to beat him considering his age and the number of breaks he took throughout the day. The older, wiser man kindly replied, "Son, what you don't understand is that every time I sat down for what you call a break, I was sharpening my ax. A well-sharpened ax makes for a lot less work, so trees fall faster."

I should conclude that story with the word *selah*, meaning, pause and think about that. The problem for so

3

many people and churches today is dull axes. People have lost the edge in their lives, their homes, their marriages, and their commitment to the Lord. Week after week we may stand in church singing the songs and lifting our hands, but there is no edge to our worship. There is no edge to the preaching. It has become just dull routine and ritual.

When you set aside time for fasting and prayer, you see greater results. Sure, you can keep cutting with a dull ax like the young man in the story, powering along in your own strength. But I would rather get more done operating under the power of God! A few days out of an entire year is not a long time, but it yields great reward. Fasting gives you back your edge. It gives you the power to do far more than you could possibly accomplish in your own strength and finite understanding.

In 2 Kings chapter 6, the prophet Elisha had acquired a group of younger men eager to be mentored by him. These so-called "sons of the prophet" had outgrown their living quarters, so they wanted to build a new, bigger building where they could all dwell and continue to be in community and learn from Elisha. Once they talked him into it, they all headed to the Jordan River, and each man began cutting down trees to make the beams for a new lodge. As they labored, one of the guys did not notice that his ax head was working loose with each powerful swing. It suddenly slipped right off of the handle and splashed into the muddy river. The iron ax head sank out of sight quickly as the young man stood on the bank, ax handle in hand, devastated and powerless to change what had just happened. He was a young man eager to do something great for God, but he could no longer help cut trees with nothing but an ax handle to swing. He had lost the edge. Furthermore, this young man had borrowed the ax, so it is likely that he was concerned that he did not have the money to replace it. Don't let lack of finances cause you to give up on your dream. Are you eager to do something great for God? Do you feel there's something more God has for you to do?

Perhaps at one time you sensed the anointing of the Lord on your life, and you were going for it. You had the edge. Your life was consecrated to God, and you had a deep passion for spiritual things. But something shifted. These days you feel like you have lost the edge. What's worse is that the enemy has convinced you that it is out of sight, out of reach, and you can never reclaim it. Have you bought the lie that your anointing, your purpose, your dream, your family, your lost children—these are all gone forever? Given the economic downturn this nation has experienced over the past several years, many have faced dire circumstances, having lost jobs, lost homes and cars, lost respect, and lost all hope. But I want to encourage you today that God can still make iron swim, and He can give you your edge back.

Make Up Your Mind

The first thing you need to do is make up your mind that you *are* going to regain your edge. I will talk more about the power of a made-up mind in the next chapter, because it is the starting point when it comes to fasting to regain your edge. But think about the young man in this story for a moment. One thing that I want to point out is his career choice. I doubt he signed up to be a woodcutter since he was pursuing the prophetic ministry! But along the way he ended up with an ax in his hand. No matter what your calling is, never turn away from hard work. Ministry is a four-letter word called W-O-R-K. Calloused hands can still pray for people! So there stood the prophet-in-training on the bank of the Jordan, not prophesying for anyone, not speaking forth any great oracles of God to the nations, just a man whose ax head flew off the handle. His word said he would be a prophet, but his world said he was a tree chopper. He could have easily just tossed the handle aside, found a stump to sit on, and given up. After all, it would be impossible to see that ax head in the muddy river. As you're reading this you may be in a season when your word doesn't match your world. Faith is trusting God no matter how impossible the odds are. Sometimes God invites us to defy the odds. Sometimes God allows the odds to be stacked against us so we can

6

experience a miracle of divine proportions through what seems to be impossible.

The impossible, however, is *exactly* what this young man signed up for! After all, he was studying under Elisha, who was later credited with twice the miracles of his predecessor Elijah. The young man was being trained and mentored by the same prophet of God who once struck that same river with Elijah's cloak and the waters immediately parted so he could walk across. This kid may have even been in the group that saw it happen. He knew that Elisha had been used to make the water of Jericho drinkable again and had made oil multiply in the widow's house. He raised a young boy from the dead and had the solution to save a batch of poisoned stew. He made bread multiply to feed a hundred men and even healed Naaman's leprosy while exposing his servant Gehazi's greed.[4] I believe this young man had made up his mind long before this incident took place that he would believe the impossible! Walking with Elisha, the impossible was part of the job. Instead of hiding away in defeat, he made the choice to hope and believe. It reminds me of a quote I read somewhere once by the founder of the Salvation Army, William Booth: "God loves with a great love the man whose heart is bursting with a passion for the impossible."

Let me remind you that as a born-again believer you serve the Lord God of Elisha! He is the Alpha and Omega, the beginning and the end.[5] Our Lord is the author and finisher of our faith.[6] He is the God of the impossible. Now is the time to make up your mind that you will believe on Him for what seems to you to be impossible and stop believing the lies of the enemy who wants to see you defeated. Step one is to make up your mind that you are going to get your edge back.

The second thing you must do to regain your edge is to confess that you have lost it. The young man did not keep silent. He immediately cried out to the prophet of God to help him regain what he had lost. You will not get anything accomplished by remaining in denial about your situation. You've probably heard the joke, "Denial is a river in Egypt." Going through religious motions day after day is no way to live. It is not what God has called you to do. If you have lost your passion, if you have lost your edge, be swift to confess it to someone who can pray with you and help you find your way back. When the young man in this story cried out, Elisha asked, "'Where did it fall?' And he showed him the place. So he cut off a stick, and threw it in there; and he made the iron float. Therefore he said, 'Pick it up for yourself.' So he reached out his hand and took it"(2 Kings 6:6–7).

The third thing you need to do is take action while the opportunity exists. Elisha did not grab the ax head for him and put it back on the handle. He had to do that for himself. God will not do for you what you can do for yourself. You would think if the iron ax head could "swim," it could have also made its way back onto the end of the ax handle. The ax head was in the river. The river represents the presence of the Holy Spirit. God intends for you to do your part in regaining the edge. When you declare a fast and set aside time for prayer, you are reaching into the river and picking up the sharp edge that God has provided for you to be effective. I challenge you to do your part. Declare a fast while you are reading this book. I'm in agreement that sharp ideas are going to come to you. Sharp relationships with new people are going to add significantly to your life. Cutting-edge creativity is going to flow your way as you begin to hunger and thirst for more.

The young prophet had to dry off that iron ax head and spend some time putting an edge back on it after it had been lost in the river. He could not just start swinging again with a dull ax, or he would not have been useful to the rest of the men in building the lodge. In the same way, losing the edge in our own lives has an impact on the lives of those around us. Do you remember the passion you had for the Lord when you were first saved? Do you remember what it was like during those first few weeks after Jesus lifted the heavy burden of sin from your life and made you clean and new? When you have that kind of passion, it is transferred to your family. Passion is transferable, but lack of passion is also transferable. The people around you notice a difference, and your passion stirs passion in their lives. However, if you have lost the edge, lost your passion, then the lack of passion is transferred. This is especially true for worship leaders, pastors, and church leaders.

The young man confessed that he had lost the edge. He cried out to Elisha and went to the spot where it was lost. We all need godly mentors in our lives, men and women of God who know how to reach out and touch heaven; a proven brother or sister who can come alongside us, hear our mistakes, and speak life and grace to help restore us. As Paul instructed the Galatian church:

> Brethren, if a man is overtaken in any trespass, you who are spiritual restore such a one in a spirit of gentleness, considering yourself lest you also be tempted. Bear one another's burdens, and so fulfill the law of Christ. For if anyone thinks himself to be something, when he is nothing, he deceives himself.
>
> —GALATIANS 6:1–3

Where did you lose it? Was it due to life's batterings and disappointments suffered along the way? I like this story that Dutch Sheets shared in his book *God's Timing for Your Life*.

> The only survivor of a shipwreck washed up on a small, uninhabited island. He cried out to God to

save him, and every day he scanned the horizon for help, but none seemed forthcoming.

Exhausted, he eventually managed to build a rough hut and put his few possessions in it. But then one day, after hunting for food, he arrived home to find his little hut in flames, the smoke rolling up to the sky. The worst had happened; he was stung with grief.

Early the next day, though, a ship drew near the island and rescued him.

"How did you know I was here?" he asked the crew.

"We saw your smoke signal," they replied.

Though it may not seem so now, your present difficulty may be instrumental to your future happiness.[7]

Let the crisis drive you to your knees in a season of prayer and fasting. Go back to the place where the edge was lost. Was it through sin that you need to confess? Go back to that place and get it under the blood of Jesus. The altar is not just for those coming to the Lord for the first time. The altar is a place to get free from that thing that weighs you down and drowns out your fiery passion for God. Alterations are made at the altar. The altar is a place to *alter* your direction and get back on the right track with God. I believe it is significant that Elisha used a stick to throw into the water. The Bible does not elaborate on this point, but to me the stick from that tree represents Calvary. When you allow the cross to touch your life afresh, when you come to the foot of the cross and confess your sin, it changes everything. Suddenly the supernatural possibilities become much more natural!

God has men and women whom He still plans to raise up in this generation—men and women who have the edge, the power of the Holy Spirit operating in their lives. If you feel dull right now, if you have lost the edge, it is time to get it back.

"This Fasting Thing Isn't for Me"

One Sunday morning before service I received a text message from Marcus Mecum, a passionate man of God who used to be on staff at Free Chapel in Georgia as our youth pastor. In 2005 he accepted the call of God and relocated his family to Florence, Kentucky, to pastor a church that had suffered rapid decline. Starting with about six hundred members, Marcus and his wife began to rebuild and reinvent the identity of that struggling congregation. Seven Hills Church is now three thousand strong, and they have seen more than four thousand people come to Christ.[8] In his e-mail, Marcus recounted his first encounter with fasting.

Ten years ago I walked into your office and said, "Pastor, this fasting thing isn't for me." You replied jokingly, "You are on staff. You're fasting." So, after some encouragement, I joined the fast. Fourteen days later, I cracked and destroyed a Whopper burger! I thought I was done. I confessed to you, and you said, "You did your best. You made it fourteen days; that's not bad." I want you to know that this January marks my tenth annual fast, and it is Seven Hills Church's sixth annual twenty-one-day fast. Knowing that people and hundreds of congregations across this nation are part of this first of the year fast and that Free Chapel helped kick-start this movement is pretty cool. I would not want anything more. (Thanks for helping me stay thinner too!)

God raised up Marcus and led him to deeper places of worship, brokenness, and power through fasting, even though his first fast was what some might call a "forced" fast. Marcus and I can still laugh about that, but I rejoice in seeing how joining the corporate fast at Free Chapel that year gave him the tools to get the edge back in his life. When you regain the edge, God is able to use you to impact others. Seven Hills was a church that had lost the edge. One of the first changes Marcus made was to begin an annual corporate fast. Lives began to change. Souls are being saved! Their website mentions that half of the four thousand new converts occurred in the past year. What thrills me even more is to know that there are hundreds of churches just like Seven Hills that the enemy tried to keep dull and powerless, but they began to fast and pray and are now beginning to get their edge back with a sharp anointing and passion for God.

Has your church lost its edge? Has your worship grown dull? Are souls being saved? Some churches begin at 11:00 a.m. sharp and end at 12:00 dull. The dead in Christ are sitting in pews, and the grave gives up her dead at noon. If this describes your service, it's time to declare a fast and pray.

More Than Food

Sometimes when you are on a fast you cannot help but think about what you will eat when the fast is over. There is nothing wrong with that (as long as you do not obsess on it so much that you lose focus and destroy a Whopper too early). But sometimes our vision and understanding are so limited. I thought about the prodigal son, the parable Jesus shared in Luke 15:11–32. You could say he was on a "forced fast" due to his bad decisions that landed him in a pigpen, sharing their rations. As hunger pangs dug at his belly the reality hit him that he did not even have corn to eat, just the dry husks! He started thinking about home and how his father's servants ate better than what he had. He planned to go home for a good meal. Little did he realize that his father had so much more in store for him than food. He welcomed his lost son home with open arms. He restored him, he clothed him, he forgave him, and he celebrated his life. The Bible tells us, "Eye has not seen, nor ear heard, nor have entered into the heart of man the things which God has prepared for those who love Him" (1 Cor. 2:9). If we could only take hold of those promises! When you fast and pray, holy surprises seem to come out of nowhere.

I met my daughter Courteney for dinner one Thursday, and she began to tell me about her friend Nate. He was not much of a churchgoer. He decided to come to Free Chapel for the first time on a Wednesday night when I preached a message titled "Jesus Passing By." My daughter said Nate texted her before he left church, telling her how much the message impacted his life. He was so moved that when he got home, he felt compelled to start reading his Bible again. A fresh passion for the Lord had been renewed in his heart. It had been months since he even picked up his Bible. In fact, it had been exactly six months. You see, six months before coming to Free Chapel that night, Nate made two thousand dollars on a job he completed. He decided to stash the cash somewhere safe, but he completely forgot where it was hidden. He searched for months but could not find the money anywhere. He finally concluded that he laid it on his car seat where it must have fallen out of the car where someone picked it up and was long gone with his money, until that Wednesday night. His heart was stirred to dig into the Word of God again, and he was completely blown away to find the two thousand dollars that was once lost tucked safely inside the pages of his Bible. God knows where your stuff is! He knows where the ax head fell off, and He will help you get your edge back.

Whenever I feel myself getting dull spiritually, I fast. It may be a short fast or a longer one, but I have learned how vital that season can be. You can get much more accomplished with a sharp ax. I look around in amazement that this church is debt free. We started with a small little building, and year after year as we have continued to put God first in all things, to press in with fasting and prayer, we have grown and paid off that growth as we expanded. Even in a slumping economy, I believe fasting and prayer opened the door to keep the ministry expanding. Fasting releases much more in your life than what you can comprehend.

Get the Trash Out

As I shared at length in my first book, *Fasting*, a spiritual fast also offers many physical health benefits. It gives the body an opportunity to cleanse itself of toxins, to become renewed and restored. Many medical doctors support the healing benefits of a fast.[9] But remember, fasting without prayer is simply a diet. Just as fasting cleanses your physical body of trash—it cleanses you spiritually as well.

Peter warned, "Be sober, be vigilant; because your adversary the devil walks about like a roaring lion, seeking whom he may devour" (1 Pet. 5:8). If you have lost your edge because of sin, it is time to get alone with God. Fasting and prayer can help you sever addictions to tobacco, to drugs, to alcohol, to pornography. Fasting and prayer help you cut out the double life, the secret sins that you believe are hidden from everyone else—but they are not hidden to God. Sin will clog the pipeline of all future blessings. Fasting is the spiritual "Drano" that unclogs the flow of the living water in our soul.

Fasting makes you sensitive to the "trash" that tries to invade your life. We don't have any movie channels on our TV because so much of it is just filth. But I was flipping through the channels one evening and was shocked to find about five movie channels available. I couldn't believe what I was seeing in my home! We called the cable company to find out what was going on. I wasn't paying for that and did not want my children stumbling across it either. The cable company explained that it was a free sixty-day trial! In other words, they pipe that stuff in unsolicited to get people hooked. Needless to say we had it taken off immediately.

You may think that is insignificant, but remember, the enemy is prowling. He is sneaking around. You hear a twig snap behind you and convince yourself that it is no big deal...but he is about to pounce. I remember the old folks saying, "The devil is in the details." What you feed your mind on matters. The kind of music you feed your soul on matters. Fasting doesn't just pertain to what you put in your stomach, but what you feed your soul and spirit as well.

Seasons of fasting and prayer help you get your sensitivity back to the things of God. When you have become dull by the constant bombardment of trash all around you, fasting helps you get the edge back to cut through the trash and clean it out. The anointing of God is precious and should not be handled as a light thing. When we begin a twenty-one-day fast at the first of the year, one of the things we always focus on is getting the trash out of the temple. The Bible says, "Do you not know that your body is the temple of the Holy Spirit who is in you, whom you have from God, and you are not your own? For you were bought at a price; therefore glorify God in your body and in your spirit, which are God's" (1 Cor. 6:19–20).

> Seasons of fasting and prayer help you get
> your sensitivity back to the things of God.

Cry out to God; fast and pray. Invite God to begin a demolition in your life. He's going to tear down who you used to be as He raises you up to become who you were meant to be, who you were born to be! God had something in mind when He put you on this earth. And I want to challenge you to whatever degree you can to make fasting part of your life.

Chapter 2

The Power of a Made-Up Mind

Time spent in fasting and prayer builds confidence and helps you develop the determination necessary to run your race with endurance. We all have need of endurance! For many years now I've enjoyed running. It has a twofold purpose for me. Running is a stress reliever, but it is also an opportunity for me to spend time in prayer. Sometimes I get so into prayer while running that I trip and fall! It's so embarrassing, especially if someone sees me. Many times I've come home from a good run with bloody knees and scraped elbows, where I tripped over a root sticking out of the ground or stumbled over a broken sidewalk. But I've learned a few secrets about going for a successful run through the years. One of them is to make up my mind before I start exactly how far I'm going to run. If I don't take that important step, my body will quickly decide that the run is over and not take any more steps. I have to prepare my mind to go the distance so that it can overrule the vote my tired muscles will cast halfway through the run. You cannot prepare to run a marathon *after* the gun has fired and the race has begun. You prepare for months, running a little further each time, conditioning your body to go the distance. In the same way, fasting and prayer prepare and condition your spirit to go the distance in life's battles.

Some people express concern, even fear, before ever attempting a fast. They are afraid they will fail, unable to stick to a fast for even one day, let alone for several days. But that changes the moment they succeed. Fear gives way to confidence. Whether you are considering a fast that lasts one day or several days, the only way to know that you *can* succeed is to make up your mind—determine in advance—that you *will* succeed, remaining faithful for the full length of the fast. Once you have succeeded at your first one-day fast, the prospect of a three-day fast becomes far less daunting because your confidence level is higher. Before long, completing a three-day fast gives you confidence to endure longer fasts as God leads. Numerous people have told me how amazed they were by the grace they experienced several days into a lengthy fast. As the writer of Hebrews encourages, "Therefore do not cast away your confidence, which has great reward. For you have need of endurance, so that after you have done the will of God, you may receive the promise" (Heb. 10:35–36). I want to endure. I want to do the will of God. I want the promise!

> Fasting and prayer prepare and condition
> your spirit to go the distance in life's battles.

Remember, fasting is not a requirement—it is a choice. Fasting does not guarantee your salvation. Fasting does not make you better than anyone else, nor does it make you some kind of religious freak. Choosing to fast is choosing to come away from the routine and wait upon the Lord with greater intensity, seeking His face and His presence in a deeper way. I have learned one of the keys to a successful fast is to make up your mind how long you are going to fast before you begin. Make a plan, write it down, and stick to it.

Choosing Your Destiny

When you get right down to it, only two things determine your destiny: your *choices* and your *responses* to God. The Word of God is full of choices. The entire twenty-eighth chapter of Deuteronomy is dedicated to choosing to do right and be blessed or to do wrong and be cursed. Moses's successor, Joshua, called upon the people of Israel to make up their minds. He gave them a simple choice: "If serving the LORD seems undesirable to you, then choose for yourselves this day whom you will serve, whether the gods your ancestors served beyond the River, or the gods of the Amorites, in whose land you are living. But as for me and my household, we will serve the LORD" (Josh. 24:15, NIV). Likewise, when the prophet Elijah challenged the prophets of Baal, he asked, "How long will you falter between two opinions? If the LORD is God, follow Him; but if Baal, follow him" (1 Kings 18:21).

An underlying theme of these choices can be summed up on the words of Romans 12:9, where Paul instructs believers, "Abhor what is evil. Cling to what is good." This theme is reflected in the life of the man named Job. The Bible describes Job as a man who "was blameless and upright, and one who feared God and shunned evil" (Job 1:1).

I believe Job made up his mind in his youth that he would serve the Lord, that he would cleave to what is good and abhor evil, and that he would stick to the narrow path. I remember when I was twelve and could not wait to turn thirteen and become an official "teenager." When you are growing up, time just drags on so slowly. When I was fifteen, I could not wait to turn sixteen and start driving. The next two years seemed to take an eternity to pass by, but finally my eighteenth birthday arrived. But suddenly time sped up. Before I knew it I was twenty-five, then thirty, forty, and at the writing of this book, nearly fifty! Decades passed by in a blur. Looking back, I am grateful for godly parents who helped me understand how to make right decisions early on in life. I look around at my wife and children whom I love; I look at the ministry where God has placed me and the influence He has given, and I know that on my own I am not qualified enough, not gifted enough, not educated enough to be doing what I am doing. Then again, it is not our giftings and education that set the course for our lives, but our choices and our responses to God.

The Lord touched my heart in a service when I was thirteen years old, and I remember making the decision that very night that I would be a virgin when I got married. I remember thinking it through and planning how I would avoid temptation in order to stick to that decision. I can still remember the day that I made up my mind that I would never touch alcohol again, that I would never touch cigarettes again. Those were not popular decisions! They were decisions that took me off the broad path where most of my friends walked, setting my course instead on the narrow path. Whenever you make a choice *against* one thing—you make a choice *for* something else. When you make up your mind to abhor evil, you make the choice to cling to what is good. In the same manner, when you choose to ignore the prompting of the Lord in an area, you are making a choice to do something that opposes His best plan for your life. My choices and my responses to God have governed my entire life. Choosing to do right is not always easy, but God's grace is sufficient to see you through.

The Day Will Come

Temptation and calamity are unavoidable. They are going to come, whether you have made up your mind how you will respond or not. Sexual temptations will confront you. If you do not have the power of a made-up mind to honor God with your body, you will be at the mercy of the lust of your flesh. The temptation to take the easy way out in a difficult situation will confront you. If you have not already made up your mind to honor God no matter the consequences, then you will most likely compromise. That is why Ecclesiastes 12 says to, "Remember now your Creator in the days of your youth, *before the difficult days come*" (v. 1, emphasis added).

There will come a day when your responses to God and the choices you have made will be tested. That day came for Job. Satan came to test him to the core. In one single day Job lost everything that he cared about and loved. His children, his servants, his herds, his properties…all destroyed in the blink of an eye. Throughout the day that faithful man of God was pummeled with one tragic story of loss and destruction following immediately on the heels of another. The final blow came in the news that all ten of his children, who were dining together at the home of his eldest son, had been killed when a windstorm destroyed the house.[1] Hearing that news:

> Then Job arose and tore his robe and shaved his head, and he fell to the ground and worshiped. And he said:
>
> "Naked I came from my mother's womb,
> And naked shall I return there.
> The LORD gave, and the LORD has taken away;
> Blessed be the name of the LORD."
>
> In all this Job did not sin nor charge God with wrong.
>
> —Job 1:20–22

That amazes me. I cannot imagine how my heart would break if something happened to just one of my children. Job immediately demonstrated the outward signs of mourning in that culture, but the powerful thing was what he demonstrated from the inside: he fell to the ground...*and worshiped.* In the face of utter calamity and loss, his heart was already prepared to worship God no matter what. Even our brokenness and great pain can be poured out on the feet of Jesus as an offering of worship.

There always comes a day of testing. That is when the value of a made-up mind truly counts. As if these horrific tragedies in one day were not enough, the enemy took a shot at Job's health too, afflicting him with painful boils from head to toe.[2] Job's wife was a hurting, grief-stricken mother who lost all of her children in a single day, and to top it off, her husband now sat on an ash heap scraping grotesque sores that covered his body. In her eyes God had abandoned them. But not in Job's eyes. Years before he had made up his mind. Back when he had his good health, when he was raising his children and watching his blessings increase, back before the testing came—he made up his mind how he would respond to God. When all was lost and his body was saying, "Give up"...when his circumstances were saying, "Throw in the towel and quit!"...when his neighbors were asking, "Where are all your kids, Job? Where are all your flocks and great wealth?"...when his wife said, "Curse God and die"...Job had endurance for the trial. He was conditioned for the marathon. When Job was younger and stronger, he responded to his Redeemer and made right choices that prepared him for the hard times so that he would not waiver in the face of such utter loss. He made up his mind that no matter what, he would praise his God.

"Abraham, where is that son you were promised? Is that him on the altar ready to be slain?"[3] Long before Abraham and Isaac walked up that mountain, Abraham had made his decision to trust and follow the Lord, his provider.

"Joseph, where is your coat of many colors? Is that it

covered with blood to convince your grieving father that you were killed by wild animals?" Joseph made up his mind to follow the Lord, the giver of dreams, long before his brothers threw him in that pit in the desert. He set his course on the narrow path before he was faced with Potiphar's scantily clad seductress of a wife, before he was falsely accused of rape and thrown into prison.[4]

"Where are those who sang songs about you being a conquering hero, David? You're out here living in a cave running for your life from King Saul even though you were anointed as the next king of Israel." David made up his mind as a young shepherd boy alone in the fields with all of heaven listening that he would serve his God.

In Daniel, chapter 1, we discover how Daniel and the three young men of Judah were taken captive into Babylon. They were to be instructed in the ways of that heathen nation, right down to eating the delicacies of the king's table, so that they could adapt and conform to the culture. "But Daniel purposed in his heart that he would not defile himself with the portion of the king's delicacies, nor with the wine which he drank" (v. 8). Instead, Daniel suggested a ten-day fast of nothing but vegetables and water to prove to the steward that he and his three friends would be in better condition than the others who ate from the king's table. At the end of the ten days the appearance of Daniel and his friends was better than the other young men, so they were given only vegetables from then on instead of the king's allotted delicacies. Circumstances did not hinder or influence Daniel's response to God. Instead of being influenced by the culture, these young men took a stand and began to influence the culture in which they found themselves.

By chapter 3, Daniel was no longer with his three friends. However, they had made up their minds not to bow the knee to any god except for the one true God of Israel. Even when faced with imminent death in the blazing furnace, the young men said, "Our God whom we serve is able to deliver us from the burning fiery furnace, and He will deliver us from your hand, O king. But if not, let it be known to you, O king, that we do not serve your gods, nor will we worship the gold image which you have set up" (Dan. 3:17–18). They watched Daniel take a stand and refuse the king's food. That lesson helped prepare them for the day that they would have to take a stand on their own. Whenever you choose to do what is right, you influence others. When you choose to fast and pray, your children learn to fast and pray. When you choose to abhor evil and cleave to good, your children, your friends, and your family learn to do so too.

"Don't Compromise"

Recently I discovered the story of Carlos Hathcock II, recognized as one of the most effective military snipers of all time, specifically during the Vietnam era. Fellow Marine Charles Henderson wrote Hathcock's amazing story in his book titled *Marine Sniper: 93 Confirmed Kills*.[5] Carlos began honing his sharpshooter skills as a young boy when he taught himself to hunt rabbit and squirrel in order to provide food for himself and his grandmother who cared for him after his parents separated. On his seventeenth birthday, Hathcock enlisted in the Marines and quickly gained notoriety by qualifying as an expert shot while in boot camp. He went on to win many shooting competitions, including the most prestigious of the long-range competitions, the Wimbledon Cup, in 1965. Then he was off to Vietnam.

His career as a Marine sniper began after a few missions with men who did not display the same knowledge of the outdoors that Hathcock had come to depend on for survival. Believing he would be safer working by himself, he quickly became the top sniper—with a total of ninety-three confirmed kills and many more unconfirmed (not witnessed) kills. Please understand that by sharing this story I am not glorifying killing. Hathcock's motivation as a sniper was simple: protect fellow Marines. He knew if he did not take out the enemy target first, Marines would die. He became so good at his job that the Vietcong (VC) put out a bounty on him for $30,000, which at that time was outrageously high. But they were desperate to eliminate the man they dubbed "*Long Tra'ng*" or "The White Feather," a nickname he earned because of the white feather he always wore in his field hat.

One enemy sniper set on collecting that bounty was diligently searching the thick jungle one day for any sign of Hathcock's white feather. From deep cover, the VC sniper scanned with his rifle's scope until he thought he saw something. As he focused in on his distant target, a glimmer of sunlight reflected off of his scope lens, alerting Hathcock of the imminent threat. Hathcock wasted no time. He raised his rifle, aimed the crosshairs where he had seen the flash, and squeezed the trigger. He and his spotter carefully approached the body to find that Hathcock's bullet had gone right through the other sniper's scope, penetrating his eye and killing him instantly. It was an unbelievable shot. The weight of the moment hit Hathcock: the only possible way for that shot to have occurred was if the enemy had him lined up in his scope as well. The only thing that saved Hathcock was that he pulled the trigger first.

That is how we live quite often as Christians, isn't it? Jesus said the enemy seeks to destroy us.[6] Like the VC sniper with Hathcock, the enemy sometimes has his "crosshairs" on us to steal, kill, and destroy. When you start impacting those around you for God, when your life starts influencing others to make choices that set their feet on the narrow path, you sometimes come under greater attack. When you fast, you are pulling the trigger first, before the crisis comes! Fasting is charging the gates of hell and ripping them off their hinges. It's a preemptive strike in spiritual warfare against the forces of darkness. That is why it is so important to have the training and discipline necessary to pull the trigger first—training and discipline that come through fasting and prayer. But there is another part of Carlos Hathcock's story that amazes me.

It was his most dangerous mission. His tour of duty was nearly over. He had saved countless lives through his unsurpassed marksmanship, skill, and determination. That is when news came that an enemy general needed to be taken out. The mission would put him deep in enemy territory with very little natural cover. He was the *only* one qualified for the mission, and even if he was to succeed, it would very likely be a mission from which he would not return alive. He would not be ordered to go; he would have to volunteer. Hathcock went over the situation in his mind. He considered how his success could turn the course of the battle significantly and spare more lives. He considered how he would not want anyone else to potentially be killed attempting what he had refused to do. He accepted the mission.

He spent the next days preparing mentally and going

over the maps and intelligence that the Marines had gathered about the lay of the land, where the general was based, his habits, and so forth. Hathcock would have to cross a large open field unseen in order to get close enough to the target to make the shot. He decided he would take aim from eight hundred yards in order to guarantee the success of the mission. Even though he was skilled from one thousand yards and farther, this mission was his most important and most dangerous. There was no room for error. He removed all of his personal items, including the trademark white feather from his cap, tucking it into his New Testament. He was flown to the drop point and left completely alone in the jungle. He then began what would become a four-day journey to cross fifteen hundred yards of that field, camouflaged and crawling like a worm, moving so slowly that his presence could not be detected by the enemy.

As the hours wore on, Hathcock inched along. By the third day, his body was covered with dozens of ant and bug bites to the point he thought even if he carried off the mission, the ants might carry off his dead carcass. His knees, hips, and elbows were covered in blisters and sores from his continual but excruciatingly slow pace. A number of times he held his breath until his lungs felt like they would burst as enemy patrols walked right past him. He had not eaten and had only taken a capful of water from his canteen often enough to stay alive. Just when it seemed things could not get much worse, he crawled within six inches of a green bamboo viper. Face-to-face with a very deadly snake, it took every ounce of restraint he had to calm himself and pray. Suddenly the snake just slithered away. Maintaining his cover, he took the next half hour to slowly inch, undetected, another capful of water from his canteen to his very dry mouth.

Pain, weariness, and hunger flooded his mind and body. Ahead of him lay two hundred more yards to crawl in order to be in perfect firing range. That is when a battle began in his mind, of which Henderson writes, "…compromise began tempting him now."

> "You can do it from here," he considered. In all his years of marksmanship competition, his best scores came from the thousand-yard line. "It's been all bull's-eyes and V's from this distance," Carlos told himself. But in all his years of shooting, never had one shot been so critical.
>
> A second voice told Carlos, "Stick to the plan. Don't change things now. Survival depends on it. Survive." Carlos always listened to that voice. It had kept him alive. "You thought out this plan when you were rested; now you're tired. Gotta stick to the plan—got to."[7]

Hathcock continued on, prompted by the advice of that "second voice." He finally reached the eight-hundred-yard point and set his position in a ditch no more than six inches deep. There he waited. The next morning when the general emerged from his bunker, Hathcock lined up his scope and reminded himself once again, "Don't compromise."[8] Going through all the variables of the shot once more, he made the necessary adjustments and squeezed the trigger. The enemy was taken out and a crucial battle was turned around because of his dedication and determination, because he did not compromise when things got difficult.

Stick to the Plan

It is so powerful to me that he reminded himself to stick to the plan he made when he was rested, when he was thinking clearly, when fatigue, fear, hunger, and pain were not in control. Long before he started across that field, he had made up his mind that there was no turning back and no room for compromise. As a Christian, fasting and praying help you build the kind of endurance you need to stay focused and victorious in battle. As you set your mind that you will not compromise during a fast, you build confidence and endurance that can carry you through the trials and battles that come. But the decisions are made long before temptation comes along. If not, it is too late. Hathcock could have thought of a dozen ways to compromise—but there was only one way to victory. There were many broad paths, but the narrow one—the one he made up his mind about when his thinking was clear—that one alone would bring success. That is why the writer of Ecclesiastes said to "remember in your youth," when your head is clear and the burdens of this life have not taken hold.

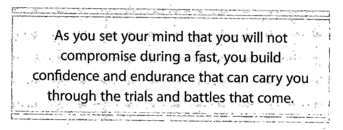

As you set your mind that you will not compromise during a fast, you build confidence and endurance that can carry you through the trials and battles that come.

Sometimes on a fast, everything in you begins to cry out for comfort: "Just one bite of cake; it's her birthday." "Just one piece of steak and I'll make it." The list of temptations goes on and on. While you must use wisdom on a fast, you must also use determination to stick to the plan. You *will* be able to make it when you stay focused on what you decided before your flesh started crying out. Pastor Mecum learned that lesson on staff at Free Chapel. After fourteen days he gave in and devoured a Whopper. Your flesh will win if your mind is not made up before you start. After that experience, however, he has completed many lengthy fasts and has seen God move in marvelous ways in his personal life and in his new church. His dedication and determination have influenced an entire congregation to fast and pray, and they are reaping the benefits.

God has a specific destiny planned for you, one that your choices and your response to Him will unlock. Any pilot can tell you where the "point of no return" is on takeoff: when all the runway has all been used up and there is no turning back—it's fly or die! There is a list of ordinary people in the eleventh chapter of the Book of Hebrews. Though ordinary, they did extraordinary things for God because they never lost the vision, and in the worst of times they refused to turn back. When you follow God, not everybody will go with you. Your dream could be their nightmare. Go with God when He is calling you out of your comfort zone. If failure is not a possibility, then success doesn't mean anything. When Abraham decided to leave home and follow God, he had no idea where that journey would take him—most likely, neither will you. I know this, however; it all begins when God starts stirring up your nest. In Deuteronomy 32:11, the writer refers to an eagle stirring its nest. The adult eagle does so to make what was once a cozy, comfortable place for the eaglets more and more uncomfortable so that they will begin to fly. Most of us are like those eaglets—until our misery factor exceeds our fear factor, we won't budge. When you start taking some risks, you will pray like you have never prayed before, and you will fast like never before, because your life depends on it! Make up your mind to

> I truly believe that fasting often accelerates your destiny.

Ecclesiastes 12 speaks of making right decisions in your youth—perhaps you feel that "youth" has passed you by. Start now. Begin today. I believe it was Thomas à Kempis, known for his famous work *The Imitation of Christ*, who said, "Lose not your confidence of making progress toward the things of the Spirit; you still have time, the hour is not yet past." Make up your mind to go after God with all your heart. Set aside times of fasting and prayer, seeking to know Him better.

Chapter 3

Wisdom Brings Success

I f fasting is the gateway through which God releases His supernatural power into our lives—why is it such an overlooked opportunity?

All the greats of the Bible fasted: Moses, David, Nehemiah, Daniel, Elijah, Paul, Peter, even Jesus Himself. They all committed themselves to a high standard of discipline to fulfill God's purposes in the earth. Fasting is telling God that you want to be with Him more than you want to spend time with other people. It is a time to focus all of your attention on Him alone. Fasting is feeding your spirit by neglecting your flesh. Most of the time we do the opposite; we neglect our spirit by feeding our flesh. Like most preachers that I know, before I preach the Word of God to a congregation, I don't eat much beforehand. I will have studied and fed my spirit on the Bread of Heaven, and after filling my spirit up, I don't want my flesh to get in the way.

Sometimes it seems like our relationship with God is

distant. Have you ever felt empty, like you were in a spiritual desert? When you get in a dry spiritual desert, one of the greatest things you can do is fast. Look at Christ's example. In the first days of His earthly ministry, Jesus went through a dry desert. However, when He fasted His way out of that dry desert place, the Bible says in Luke 4:14, "He returned in the power of the Spirit." Fasting will ignite the power of the Holy Spirit within you. After the fast had ended, Jesus encountered a demon-possessed man and set him free. When you fast, God will send difficult cases your way because, through the wilderness experience of fasting, you've become more prepared and equipped for ministry. God wants you to minister to people He sends across your path who need to be encouraged and set free. Prayer is not always enough. As Jesus said in Mark 9:29, "This kind can come out by nothing but prayer and fasting." Sometimes deliverance requires both prayer and fasting.

Hell Is Not in Charge

Have you ever wondered why Jesus fasted before He started His ministry on Earth? Jesus is called the Son of Man and the Son of God. He was all man and all God in one form. Jesus said, "Most assuredly, I say to you, the Son can do nothing of Himself, but what He sees the Father do; for whatever He does, the Son also does in like manner" (John 5:19). He also said, "I and My Father are one" (John 10:30). That is about as close as any two beings can get. But, even though He was God's Son and He and the Father were "one," we also know that before Jesus began His earthly ministry, He was led by the Holy Spirit into the desert on a forty-day fast.

> When He had been baptized, Jesus came up immediately from the water; and behold, the heavens were opened to Him, and He saw the Spirit of God descending like a dove and alighting upon Him. And suddenly a voice came from heaven, saying, "This is My beloved Son, in whom I am well pleased." Then Jesus was led up by the Spirit into the wilderness to be tempted by the devil. And when He had fasted forty days and forty nights, afterward He was hungry.
>
> —MATTHEW 3:16–4:2

Fasting has been a lifestyle for me since I was about seventeen years old. I watched my father, a faithful man of God, model fasting and prayer when I was growing up. I have been on short fasts and long fasts, but I have to be honest and say that I do not know how Jesus fasted for that long *in the wilderness*. It is difficult enough to complete a twenty-one-day fast with all of today's comforts like heat, air conditioning, and a comfortable bed to sleep in at night. Imagine our Savior, our King, fasting for that long in the wilderness of Israel, with no water, no food, no bed, and being constantly nagged by the devil. It makes me think of the words of David when he was in the desert of Judah

> O God, You are my God;
> Early will I seek You;
> My soul thirsts for You;
> My flesh longs for You
> In a dry and thirsty land
> Where there is no water.

—Psalm 63:1

Notice that David did not say he thirsted for water in the desert, but for God. I have been to Israel and walked through some of the desert regions there. The wilderness there is a harsh climate of extremes. It gets very dry and hot during the day like the inside of an electric clothes dryer set on high. The nights can become very cold and dark. Yet before Jesus started His earthly ministry, the Holy Spirit led Him into that extreme setting to fast and pray for you and for me and for His purpose on Earth.

I wonder if Jesus would have succeeded over the enemy in that wilderness if He had not fasted. With the water of the Jordan River still running down His face and clothes, God's voice was heard declaring Jesus to be His Son, in whom He was well pleased.[1] What better time to launch a public ministry than when God Himself publicly proclaims His pleasure in you! That is how man typically

43

chooses to do things—in his own strength. But instead of having crowds of devoted followers clamoring about, Jesus went into total isolation for forty days and nights, eating nothing and being tempted by the devil the entire time. The Bible does not detail the temptations Jesus endured during the fast, only those that came at the end of it. I would imagine most of the temptations during the fast were intended to get Him to quit the fast.

It never fails. When you decide that you are going to fast for a day, a week, or longer, food becomes more of a temptation than ever. You declare a fast on Sunday. Monday morning at work some generous soul decides to stop and buy doughnuts and sausage biscuits to share with everyone at the office. Perhaps it is the boss's birthday, so someone orders pizza and a huge birthday cake. One year during our annual twenty-one-day fast, my wife and my two sisters treated my mother to P.F. Chang's for her birthday. While they were enjoying a totally vegetarian meal in keeping with the fast, a waiter came to their table and placed a steaming fresh platter of Mongolian beef right in the center. They protested that they had not ordered the dish, but to their complete surprise the waiter replied, "Oh, there's no confusion, ladies. This dish is compliments of the chef." My family has eaten at that same restaurant numerous times before (when not on a fast) without ever receiving a dish like that from the chef. My wife's reaction was classic. While she truly appreciated the kind gesture from the chef, she also recognized the source of temptation. She looked at my sisters and mother and said jokingly, "That was nothing but the devil!" Needless to say, they did not partake of the Mongolian beef that day.

He Knows—Do You?

Jesus was led by the Spirit to fast and pray in that desert before He preached one sermon, healed one cripple, freed one captive, or called one disciple. All the while He was sharpening His ax for what was yet to come. As the writer of Ecclesiastes stated, "wisdom brings success" (Eccles. 10:10). At the end of those forty long days and nights in the desert, Satan tested Jesus in three specific areas intended to get Jesus to compromise the path to our redemption. Satan did not want Jesus to succeed at taking back what Adam and Eve had turned over to him when they gave in to their appetites and ate from the tree of the knowledge of good and evil.[2]

Satan first tested the Lord in His fleshly appetites: "If You are the son of God, command that these stones become bread" (Matt. 4:3). Notice he said, "If." He challenged Jesus's identity. It would have been easy for Him to turn stones into bread. God had made manna fall from heaven and water come forth from a rock in the desert when Israel wandered for forty years. Surely "if" Jesus was the Son of God, He could make bread out of stone and satisfy His intense hunger. But Jesus was not interested in bread that fills the stomach and sustains the body for a little while. He was the Bread of Life—to be broken for us. He resisted the temptation, saying, "It is written: 'Man shall not live on bread alone, but on every word that comes from the mouth of God'" (v. 4, NIV).

If you are born again, Satan knows who you are in Christ. He knows the covenant that you have was made with the blood of Jesus. He knows that you have authority over all of his power. But he does not have to recognize who you are in Christ as long *you* do not recognize who you are in Christ—all he has to do is tempt you and lead you by your fleshly appetites. We are driven by our flesh far more often than we should be. We want what we want when we want it, and we want it *now!* Fasting "dethrones" the rule of our demanding fleshly appetites so that we can more easily follow the leading of the Holy Spirit.

Jesus said we must not live on bread alone but on every *word* from the mouth of God. "Word" translated from the original Greek in that passage means the uttered, revealed, spoken word of God. Think about that…forty days earlier God the Father uttered the words, "This is my beloved Son, in whom I am well pleased." I believe that powerful *rhema word* sustained Jesus through forty days without food, and even through the hours of temptation after that long fast! That rhema word was like freshly baked bread in our Lord's mouth, so much so that Jesus had no need to prove Himself by turning old stones into bread. That rhema word had proclaimed His identity for even the devil to hear!

No Shortcuts

When Satan approached Jesus a second time at the end of that fast, he led Him up to the highest point in Jerusalem and told Jesus to jump off. Satan quoted from Psalm 91: "For he will command his angels concerning you to guard you in all your ways; they will lift you up in their hands, so that you will not strike your foot against a stone" (vv. 11–12, NIV). Two key things were at work in that temptation. The first challenges the truth of what God said in His Word, to which Jesus answered, "It is also written: 'Do not put the Lord your God to the test'" (Matt. 4:7, NIV).

> Fasting "dethrones" the rule of our demanding fleshly appetites so that we can more easily follow the leading of the Holy Spirit.

The second element reveals that Satan knew Jesus came to die. That was His purpose. So Satan was tempting the Lord to get on with it sooner, to shortcut the process.

Unfortunately that is a temptation that still trips up many believers today. We do not want to endure the process, we do not want to battle the extremes, we do not want the sharpening of the wilderness, of rejection, of isolation. Too many desire to go directly from promise to possession, and they are simply not ready. But there are seasons we simply must go through if we are ever going to be able to receive the things that God desires to download into our lives.

The people of Israel were tired of foreign rule and oppression. They were looking for a bold ruler, not someone hidden away in the desert fasting and praying. People probably saw this fast as a setback. It is certainly not how most people would take over the world. But remember, every setback you have encountered...every time God said no when you thought He should say yes...every time things have gone wrong and you just did not understand—God was shaping you. He was molding you and training you, developing your faith and trust in Him. When Jesus refused that temptation, the devil returned with one more.

Adam and Eve lost the dominion they had been given because of what they ate. Jesus started taking back that dominion because He fasted. The final temptation in that wilderness almost made sense.

> Again, the devil took him to a very high moun-
> tain and showed him all the kingdoms of the

world and their splendor. "All this I will give you," he said, "if you will bow down and worship me." Jesus said to him, "Away from me, Satan! For it is written: 'Worship the Lord your God, and serve him only.'" Then the devil left him, and angels came and attended him.

—MATTHEW 4:8–11, NIV

There is always enough truth mingled in with Satan's lies to make them nearly believable. The truth is, what he offered Jesus was his to give at that moment. He could have spared Jesus the betrayal of Judas, the deep wounding of His flesh as He was scourged, and ultimately, the gruesome and torturous death on the cross. Satan wanted Jesus to skip fasting, to skip three years in ministry, to skip the cross—to take a shortcut. But there were no shortcuts to be taken.

Sometimes God makes a promise that requires a process. So often we want the promise, but we do not want to go through God's process to get us there. Jesus went through a process of fasting forty days to prepare Him for ministry. That was one part of the process that paved the way for God's promise to be fulfilled through the cross. I'm thankful every day that Jesus didn't take the shortcut, that He went through the process to get to the promise.

Are you living a lifestyle that doesn't allow you to stop

and listen to God? Has the unspoken attitude of your heart become one of, "If God has anything to say, He better hurry up and say it"? God is saying to you today "You will seek Me and find Me, when you search for Me with all your heart" (Jer. 29:13). Intimacy cannot be rushed. It must be worked on day by day. Jesus was often surrounded by crowds of people, but He often withdrew to get alone with God and pray. He knew that He needed to stay tapped into the Source of all things, and so do we. There is a price to be paid for hearing from God and walking in His will.

Prayer and fasting were a big part of Jesus's life. Why should it be such a small part of yours? The problem with most of us is we are too impatient. If God doesn't speak to us in the first five minutes of prayer, we decide He isn't talking today. Where is the tenacity of the old saints who would take hold of God in prayer and fasting and refuse to let go until they received a sure word, a rhema word? We have been blighted with a microwave mentality, but we serve a Crock-Pot God. We want everything overnight, including maturity. We've deleted from our Bibles the scriptures that command us to wait upon the Lord. Jesus was waiting on God for forty days and nights as He fasted in the wilderness. God was working on Him. There is a work going on in you right now that you may not be fully aware of, but without fasting, prayer, and wilderness experiences, you will never be qualified to handle what

God has for you in the future. Fasting prepares you for what is yet to come!

> Prayer and fasting were a big part of Jesus's life. Why should it be such a small part of yours?

Fifteen times in the New Testament the Lord says, "He who has an ear, let him hear what the Spirit says." That tells you three important things about hearing. First, you were born into God's family with spiritual ears. The old CB radio operators would call out to each other, saying, "Have you got your ears on, good buddy?" God is asking us the same! Secondly, however, having spiritual ears to hear from God is not enough. You also have to learn to use them. A baby is born with the ability to hear but doesn't understand what he is hearing. Understanding takes time. It takes intimacy with the parents. Before Jesus ascended into heaven, Luke records that "He opened their understanding, that they might comprehend the Scriptures" (Luke 24:45). They had been hearing the Scriptures all their lives but still did not fully understand them until then. And thirdly, hearing from God must become the highest priority of your life. Why is it that we can hear from God in crisis better than other times? Because we have to. A crisis moves hearing from God to priority number one. But until hearing from Him is always our first priority, we will keep living from crisis to crisis and never learn to hear from Him correctly. Fasting is slowing down to speed up. It's taking time to listen for your next set of instructions from the throne.

There Is Work to Be Done

The wisdom of coming away with the Lord and sharpening our ax indeed brings success. We see it modeled in the life of Jesus more than once. If Jesus needed the power of the Holy Spirit in His life and ministry on Earth, then you and I need that same power all the more. The days are not getting any easier. The church desperately needs to regain the edge for the battles ahead. We need the power of the Holy Spirit operating in our lives. The words of the great Christian missionary Hudson Taylor bring this need into clear focus:

> But has the whole Church ever, since the days before Pentecost, put aside every other work and waited for Him for ten days, that that power might be manifested? Has there not been a source of failure here? We have given too much attention to methods and to machinery and to resources, and too little to the Source of Power—the filling with the Holy Ghost.[3]

Hudson Taylor knew by experience the power of God and the influence it had through his work and ministry laboring in China. He founded China Inland Ministries in 1865 and broke new ground into that closed country. He began a lasting work that still impacts lives today. In the days before Pentecost, the church waited upon the promise of God.

The Holy Spirit knows when we need to fast and pray. It is beyond my ability to even fathom what great things could be wrought on this earth if God's people would heed the Spirit's voice and follow His leading. We rarely desire to be in the extremes of the wilderness, but the same Holy Spirit who leads us into blessings can also lead us to the desert to come away for a season of fasting and prayer. The thing to remember is if He is leading, He is *with* you! There are seasons when we will be led by the Holy Spirit into a time of self-denial, when we interrupt the routine of our life and go into a time of isolation alone with God.

On that forty-day wilderness fast Jesus modeled for us the fact that sometimes you must get away from everything else and put your flesh under submission. Christians cry out, "God, use me. God, I want Your purposes manifest in my life." We are so anxious to cut down trees, but we must learn to take the time necessary to sharpen the ax. Fasting is not fun. There is not a lot of joy during a fast—but I can assure you there is joy afterward. As we see in Hebrews 4:15–16, "For we do not have a High Priest who cannot sympathize with our weaknesses, but was in all points tempted as we are, yet without sin. Let us therefore come boldly to the throne of grace, that we may obtain mercy and find grace to help in time of need." Jesus knew the secret of spending time fasting and praying in the presence of God to find mercy and grace to endure.

The power of the Holy Spirit is the edge we need to endure. Jesus sent the Holy Spirit to dwell *with* us and to dwell *in* us to lead and empower us to do the greater works He prepared for us to do.[4] One thing that I believe all Christians must come to realize is if we are going to walk with God, at some point we need to get out of our comfort zone. Life brings extremes. Is the Spirit of God leading you into a season of fasting? Follow Him! You will "return in the power of the Spirit" with a fresh rhema word from God for your life. We want everything with a shortcut, but remember there is work to be done. His timing is perfect, and your time will come.

Chapter 4

The Fast I Have Chosen

My sister has four wonderful children. She decided to begin a six-day fast—one day for each of her kids, the fifth day for her husband, and the sixth day for our mother who was going through a particularly difficult season. Each day as she fasted, my sister set aside time in prayer for the person for whom that day was dedicated. She prayed that their hearts would remain tender before the Lord. She prayed over their futures and for their divine destinies to be discovered and fulfilled. As she fasted and prayed each day, she spent time waiting to hear what was on God's heart for each person, and then she prayed according to what the Holy Spirit impressed upon her heart.

About the time her fast ended, when I asked my sister how she was doing, she looked at me for a moment, and then I watched the biggest tears gently overflow her beautiful blue eyes. In a quiet voice, she said of her tears, "This is all I can do. This is *all* I can do."

I said, "Then the fast is working."

How I wish there were a way to convey in words how amazing it is when you enter into that secret place with God through fasting and prayer. It may be difficult on the flesh temporarily, but the long-term reward far outweighs the short-term cost. My sister's season of fasting not only stored up vital prayers for her children, her husband, and our mother—but it also brought her deeper into the presence of God where a fresh brokenness in worship filled her literally to overflowing. We must grasp the concept that it is not until we are truly broken and spilled out that we can be filled to overflowing.

Brokenness is so precious in the eyes of the Lord. One of the things that I deeply desire for God to do in my own life and in the life of everyone at Free Chapel is to bring a true spirit of brokenness to our worship. Most of us struggle with the concept that it is our own strength that draws God's attention, when our strength is the very *last* thing God notices. God responds to brokenness, but not so He can rush in and save the day like some kind of cartoon hero. Brokenness makes room for Him to release His strength through our weakness in order to accomplish His plans. That is a crucial difference that we need to understand.

When God sent Samuel to anoint a new king to replace Saul as the leader of Israel, He guided Samuel past all the older, stronger, more experienced sons of Jesse, young men who by all appearances seemed well suited to be king.[1] But

God told Samuel not to look at the boys' outer appearance or their physical strength. God refused them, saying, "The LORD does not see as man sees; for man looks at the outward appearance, but the LORD looks at the heart" (1 Sam. 16:7). It wasn't strength or stature that God required, nor was it their willingness to go with Samuel to church that day. None of those boys spent hours alone with God the way that their little brother David did; none of them sang to God in the dark hours of the night with none to listen but a few restless sheep...and heaven. Samuel was instructed to call for David and anoint him as the king God had chosen for Himself because David had a heart for God, a brokenness that God could fill.

Remember the story of God speaking to Moses from the burning bush? It's found in chapters 3 and 4 of the Book of Exodus. God disrupted Moses's daily routine with a sight he had never seen before, a big bush that was on fire but was not consumed by the flames. When Moses made a point to stop what he was doing, turn, and investigate, God began to speak with him.

> Brokenness makes room for God to release His strength through our weakness in order to accomplish His plans. That is a crucial difference that we need to understand.

Forty years earlier Moses fled Egypt a broken and confused man. His pride and zeal had led him to murder an Egyptian who was beating a fellow Hebrew. By the next day Moses's own people had turned on him, as did the king of Egypt, who desired to kill him. He escaped into the desert where he later married, started a family, and began herding sheep. He buried himself in his new identity and profession, right down to the shepherd's rod that he carried at all times. That rod was not only a tool, but it also symbolized what he did and who he was, his security. Even so, it was just a dead stick. God had the needs of a bigger flock in mind when He stopped Moses that day, the day Moses's brokenness was complete.

The cries of the Hebrew people had come to the attention of the Lord. It was time to commission and equip Moses to carry out His plan to deliver the people of Israel from the oppressive bondage of slavery in Egypt. Moses couldn't fathom how in the world his Hebrew brethren would ever believe him. He questioned how God could possibly use him with all his limitations and his horrible past. So God instructed Moses to throw down the rod he held in his hand. When he dropped that stick, releasing that symbol of his identity and his own strength, God gave him a startling demonstration of His ability to work with even a dead stick in order to serve His purposes! Moses, a broken man, was filled with the power and presence of the Lord, and the people in bondage were set free.

What are God's purposes in the earth today?

Are people in bondage today, desperate for freedom and an end to the torture and suffering, crying out to a God they don't even know? Does He desire to use us to break their chains? Yes and yes! The real question is, Will you and I interrupt our lives and our routines—even our religious routines—enough to regain the edge and truly become broken before the Lord so that He can use us to reach them? It is not a coincidence that the meekest man in the Bible was one who fasted. Moses fasted for forty days, and God used him to lead His people to freedom.

The Real Deal

Fasting is not just another religious exercise. In fact, if you read Isaiah 58 carefully, you see that the chapter actually begins with God rebuking the people who were fasting because their form of fasting was merely a mundane outward display to demonstrate their religiosity. Of their hypocrisy God said:

> Is such a fast as yours what I have chosen, a day for a man to humble himself with sorrow in his soul? [Is true fasting merely mechanical?] Is it only to bow down his head like a bulrush and to spread sackcloth and ashes under him [to indicate a condition of heart that he does not have]?

Will you call this a fast and an acceptable day to
the Lord?

—Isaiah 58:5, amp

God saw right through that religious fast as just
another routine! Fasting is supposed to break the routine,
not become another passionless performance. The
Amplified Bible uses the term "bulrush" in this passage,
referring to a tall, grassy reed that grew along rivers. It
was hollow on the inside, so it would easily bow down
with its own weight, similar in appearance to someone
bowing down in hollow humility. It reminds me of the
mechanical bulls that became popular in the 1980s. They
were originally designed for rodeo riders to use for practice, but they quickly caught on as a form of entertainment for "wannabe" cowboys and cowgirls everywhere.
Even though those things can be engineered to imitate
nearly all the moves of a real bucking bull—they are only
mechanical. They go through the motions, but they're not
the real deal.

God is looking for the real deal! If we are not careful,
every one of us can grow hardened to the Spirit of God
and indifferent in our worship, mechanically going
through the motions with no brokenness, no passion. It
is easy for Christians to cruise along through life in a dull
routine. I've learned that it is dangerous to have a growing
ministry and at the same time have shrinking passion

for God. It is dangerous for whatever your focus is to get bigger on the outside, while inside your passion for God has grown cold. Perhaps you added another zero to your salary this year…but there was a time when you didn't have anything and tears would flow as you worshiped. The more He does for us, the more thankful we should be— not the more relaxed and comfortable. If you are cruising along in a dull, passionless routine, it is time to break the routine. That's what fasting—true fasting—does. Fasting clears the way for us to refocus and hear the heart of God. As I've said before, fasting is a short-term discipline that yields long-term effects. Fasting is a choice you and I can make to interrupt "life as usual" in order to hear what God wants to do and how He wants to use us to make a difference in someone else's life.

> I've learned that it is dangerous to have a growing ministry and at the same time have shrinking passion for God.

Men, women, and children desperately cry out for help every day, all over the world, in this country, perhaps even right down the street. They are in bondage. They are abused, oppressed, misused, hungry, alone, forgotten, and crushed. We may not be able to hear their cries—but you can believe that God does. He hears the cry of the oppressed and the unsaved. That is why the fast God desires is not an empty, passionless religious act that bears no fruit. God cannot bless that. God has a specific purpose for fasting and prayer.

> Is this not the fast that I have chosen:
> To loose the bonds of wickedness,
> To undo the heavy burdens,
> To let the oppressed go free,
> And that you break every yoke?
> Is it not to share your bread with the hungry,
> And that you bring to your house the poor who
>   are cast out;
> When you see the naked, that you cover him,
> And not hide yourself from your own flesh?
> Then your light shall break forth like the
>   morning,
> Your healing shall spring forth speedily,
> And your righteousness shall go before you;
> The glory of the Lord shall be your rear guard.
> Then you shall call, and the Lord will answer;
> You shall cry, and He will say, "Here I am."
>
> If you take away the yoke from your midst,
> The pointing of the finger, and speaking
>   wickedness,
> If you extend your soul to the hungry
> And satisfy the afflicted soul,
> Then your light shall dawn in the darkness,

And your darkness shall be as the noonday.
The LORD will guide you continually,
And satisfy your soul in drought,
And strengthen your bones;
You shall be like a watered garden,
And like a spring of water, whose waters do not
    fail.

—ISAIAH 58:6–11

I know people who have experienced tremendous blessings in their lives, their families, their marriages, their finances, and their businesses as they have developed a faithful lifestyle of fasting and prayer. But there is so much more that God desires to do beyond our own borders and needs! The brokenness that comes through fasting starts with throwing everything we identify as our strength down at the feet of Jesus to say, "Lord, I know I am limited. I'm coming to You in brokenness, not in my strength but in my weakness. I acknowledge that You can do more through me, broken, than I can ever attempt to do on my own." That is the type of fasting that connects with God.

Life Speakers

I was on a fast when the Lord birthed the vision for the Life Speakers ministry in my heart. I was becoming increasingly aware of the horrific nature of human trafficking—modern-day slavery—in all its forms, from forced labor to child sex trafficking. The growing statistics are inconceivable. The US State Department indicates that 12.3 million adults and children are trapped in modern slavery worldwide.[2] According to UNICEF, more than 2 million children are trapped in the global commercial sex trade.[3] Human trafficking has risen to such a level in the United States and the world that it is becoming the second highest crime after drug trafficking.[4] The more broken my heart became for the victims of the sex-slave trade, the more I knew that I couldn't do everything—but I could do *something*. During the fast the Holy Spirit brought the scripture to mind from Ezekiel, where God showed the prophet a valley full of dried-out bones that were scattered as far as the eye could see. God then told Ezekiel, "Prophesy to these bones, and say to them, 'O dry bones, hear the word of the LORD! Thus says the Lord GOD to these bones: "Surely I will cause breath to enter into you, and you shall live"'" (Ezek. 37:4–5). Victims of trafficking are like dry bones; they are sapped of all hope, joy, and life, like the walking dead. But God has a plan—and He is looking for brokenness so that He can show Himself strong. As Scripture says in 2 Chronicles 16:9, "The eyes of the LORD run to and fro throughout the whole earth, to show Himself strong on behalf of those whose heart is loyal to Him."

The Lord opened doors for us to link arms with ministries like Pastor Matthew Barnett's Dream Center to help them open a wing at the center that will be dedicated to the rehabilitation of women and young girls who have been rescued from this horrific form of slavery. We began working with Philip Cameron and his ministry in Moldova that was established to rescue young girls who age-out of state-run orphanages at sixteen years of age and quickly become victims of waiting traffickers. We are also working with Christine Caine and The A21 Campaign, which stands in the gap to rescue young girls from sex trafficking in Greece. Together we are working to help rescue women and children from predators and then helping to feed and clothe them. We are giving them safe shelter where they can find healing and even learn life skills they will need to succeed on their own. Most importantly, we share with them the love of God and the message of the gospel. In less than two years we have been able to give millions of dollars toward this cause. My oldest daughter has gone and worked the front lines at these ministries and has been profoundly impacted by the suffering she witnessed. We are following God's instruction to take our bread and resources and feed the poor and break their chains. God can do a great deal with brokenness.

What "good works" does God have for you to do, that

you'll discover only during a fast, where brokenness makes way for the grace and equipping you need?

It may be the difference you make in just one life— or you may find that He is using you to make a difference in millions of lives. Brokenness opens a door and makes a way where there seems to be no way. As Jesus said, "Most assuredly, I say to you, unless a grain of wheat falls into the ground and dies, it remains alone; but if it dies, it produces much grain. He who loves his life will lose it, and he who hates his life in this world will keep it for eternal life. If anyone serves Me, let him follow Me; and where I am, there My servant will be also. If anyone serves Me, him My Father will honor" (John 12:24–26).

Room for More

Think about what took place when Jesus and the disciples traveled through Samaria on their way to Galilee.[5] They stopped at the well in the Samarian town of Sychar. The disciples were hungry, so they went into the city to buy some food, but Jesus decided to stay at the well. When a local woman walked up to get some water, Jesus asked her for water. Since Jews didn't speak to Samaritans, that was the first thing that surprised the woman about Him. But it wasn't the last. Jesus began to tell her things about her life, like how many times she had been married and the fact that the man she currently lived with was not her husband. The Lord's insights into her life prompted her to acknowledge that He must be a prophet, so she responded as so many of us tend to do: she started religious discussion in the hopes of deflecting His attention off of her. She hoped that turning the discussion to the long-standing debate between Samaritans and Jews over whether one must worship in Jerusalem or on the mountain in Samaria where her people had worshiped since the time of Jacob would do the trick. But again Jesus brought the attention back to her and the fact that she was not worshiping at either location with her whole heart. He told her, "The hour is coming, and now is, when the *true worshipers* will worship the Father in spirit and truth; for the Father is seeking such to worship Him. God is Spirit, and those who worship Him must worship in spirit and truth" (John 4:23–24, emphasis added).

The disciples came back about that time, and though they wondered why Jesus was going against custom to talk to a woman, they chose not to ask. When Jesus told the woman that He was the Messiah, she got too excited to care about getting water from the well. She left her jar behind as she ran into town telling everyone what she'd just experienced. Samaritans only followed the first five books of the Bible. They didn't yet have the whole truth. But they were hungry. They desired more. When the men of her town heard her words, they went out to see Jesus for themselves.

Notice that when the disciples went to town, they didn't bring back someone who needed to be healed. They didn't bring back someone they had raised from the dead or a demoniac they had set free. The only thing they brought back was lunch. When the Samaritan woman went to town, the whole town followed her back! The disciples brought Jesus a Happy Meal, but she brought Him souls! I like what Hudson Taylor said about her: "Some are jealous of being successors of the Apostles. I would rather be a successor of the Samaritan woman, who—while the Apostles went for meat and forgot souls—forgot her water pot in her zeal to spread the good tidings."[6] As more people from the town gathered around Jesus, the disciples encouraged the Lord to eat. "But He assured them, I have food (nourishment) to eat of which you know nothing and have no idea....My food (nourishment) is to do the will (pleasure) of Him Who sent Me and to accomplish and completely finish His work" (John 4:32, 34, AMP). While the disciples wanted to fill their bellies with food, God wanted to fill a city with revival.

Some of our churches have become like that today—we have no room for more. We sit and receive until we are full to our ears, belching in our "La-Z-Boy" pews with our "remote controls" flipping through what we do and don't like in a service, so stuffed that we have no room for more and no passion for Jesus. If the twelve apostles could miss it, you and I are certainly capable of taking for granted the goodness of the Lord. We can easily become so full of ourselves that we must be emptied through fasting and prayer, seeking the Lord in brokenness. I believe with all of my heart that God is looking for people who will not lose their passion—people He can bless in abundance, and the more He blesses them, the hungrier, the more passionate they will become and the more kingdom power will be released as a result.

It is amazing to me that everything Jesus endured through His trial, through His beating, through His crucifixion—is called His *passion*. Power follows passion! That applies to so many areas. If you are standing in a worship service and it doesn't seem to have any power, remember that power follows passion. Is there any passion in the worship, or is it just routine? Is there any passion in the preaching, or is it another dull sermon? When one person can break through with passion, power can be released. If you are guilty of holding the "remote control" at times because you don't like the song, you don't like the music, you don't sense any passion in the worship, throw out the remote and bring the passion yourself—I believe you will see a difference!

Where there is hunger, there is passion. Where there is passion, there is power. Whenever we see the release of power in the Bible, it follows someone not caring what others thought. Remember the blind man, Bartimaeus, who cried out to Jesus amidst the rebuke of the crowd?[7] Remember the woman with the issue of blood, who risked everything by pressing through that crowd of people to just touch the Lord's robe?[8] Remember Mary, anointing the feet of Jesus? She didn't care what the others thought of her when she came to the place where Jesus was eating. She knelt at his feet, broke open a vial of expensive fragrant oil, and lavishly poured out her worship over Him. She used her own hair to wipe excess oil from His feet. The disciples ridiculed her, complaining about the waste, some pointing out the sins of her past life, but Jesus rebuked them all on her behalf.[9] Not only did Jesus have the aroma of the anointing on Him, but Mary did also. When you spend time in broken worship with Jesus, what's on Jesus will rub off on you. You can't truly pour out your worship on Jesus without some of the fragrance of that anointing coming back on you. It is what happens when you spend time in broken worship. It should be your desire to have said of you what was said of the disciples: "They recognized that they had been with Jesus" (Acts 4:13, AMP).

What God Chooses

Lou Engle, in his audiobook *Nazirite DNA*, said, "It is worth it all to separate yourselves from the addictions to

sports, the addictions to food, and the addictions to entertainment, just to know the extreme pleasures of God's love
and to fulfill the prophetic destiny He has placed upon
your lives to shape history with Him."[10] That is what the
fast that God has chosen does. It breaks the bondages
and limitations off of your life so that God can release
His power through you to others. Fasting is an inten-
tional choice to press into the depths of God's heart to
hear His plans and move forward in your divine destiny
in the power of His Spirit.

God chooses a fast that loosens bonds of wickedness,
lifts heavy burdens, frees those who are oppressed, and
breaks every yoke. Do you feel like something has been
holding you back from your destiny? Do you live with the
weight of depression or discouragement…with the burden
of providing for your family in a shaky economy…with
the pressure of children who are not saved? As you fast,
cry out to the Lord to break those bonds, to lift those
burdens that make you feel hopeless and helpless. Let
Him put the pieces back together in your own life—it is
one of the rewards of fasting. Soon you will see Him use
you to bring freedom to others as well.

Is there something in your life that has you bound,
weighed down, and held back? Are you "yoked" to a
bad habit, an iniquity, a habitual sin? A yoke was a hard
wooden implement used around the neck of two oxen to
harness one to the other for plowing. Where one ox went,

the other ox had to move with him. Are you yoked to something that is destroying your life? Do you have bad habits that are keeping you in bondage, hindering your health, shortening your life, and destroying your Christian witness? You don't have to remain yoked to your addictions. The fast God chooses breaks every yoke!

Have you ever been on an airplane when they give the safety instructions? The flight attendant always explains how the oxygen masks will fall from overhead compartments. She or he will then explain that you are to put the mask on yourself *first* before trying to assist someone else. That is what God desires—for you to come in a position of brokenness in fasting so that He can break every yoke of bondage and lift every burden off of your life *first*, so that He can then empower you to rescue others…to feed the hungry, to house the poor and the outcasts, and to clothe the naked.

The fast God chooses gives revelation to areas that have been clouded in your life as He communicates His will and direction for your life. Your light will break forth, and the Lord promises to guide you continually. God is going to provide for you! Quit worrying and start fasting.

Nothing Wasted

Do you feel like it's all just a waste of time because you have wasted far too much of your life for God to do anything through you? Maybe you think that of a loved one whom you have tried for years to reach. I want to make it perfectly clear that you are perfectly wrong in that thinking. In God's hands nothing is wasted. The Bible says the prodigal son "gathered up all that he had and journeyed into a distant country, and there he wasted his fortune in reckless and loose [from restraint] living" (Luke 15:13, AMP). But the day came when there was the return of the waster. He came to his senses, and his father restored him completely. Have you spent your life wasted on drugs, on alcohol? Have you wasted your years by abusing your body with sexual addictions? Fasting can break the yoke of the waster. It takes courage to say, "I have an addiction in my life, and I need to be free." But Jesus knows that you have wasted enough of your life, and it is time to be made completely new. If you are struggling with an addiction, fast and pray…seek the Lord in your brokenness. Nothing is hidden from His sight. Just as He knew everything about the woman at the well, He knows everything about you. But if you will allow yourself to become broken and spilled out before Him, He can cleanse you. He can fill you with His love. He will remove that burden and repair what has been wasted.

Even after Jesus fed the multitudes all they could eat by multiplying a few small loaves of bread and some fish, He told the disciples to "gather up now the fragments (the broken pieces that are left over), so that nothing may be lost and wasted" (John 6:12, AMP). Maybe you know someone who is hooked on drugs, alcohol, or some other kind of vice. I urge you to set aside the burger and cry out to God on their behalf instead. Gather up the fragments of that person's wasted life as you fast and pray for his or her deliverance. God wants nothing wasted! Is your life cluttered with fragments and broken pieces? Take them to the Lord. Lay them at His feet. Let Him restore and rebuild and fill you with His passion. God cares about the fragments and pieces of your life!

If you are a parent, has the enemy convinced you that you have never had a good relationship with your kids, you never will, and it's a waste of time to try? Or maybe he's whispered that you will never mend the relationship with your parents, your spouse, or your siblings because too much stuff has been said and been done. You have become convinced that the hurt runs so deep that they will never speak to you again. I believe when you fast according to what God calls a fast, you will "not hide yourself from your own flesh" (Isa. 58:7). In other words, the walls that have divided you will crumble as every wall of resistance begins to weaken. While you fast and pray, ask God to restore what the enemy has taken from your family. Pray that lines of communication that have been destroyed between your own flesh-and-blood relatives will be restored.

Of the fast He chooses, God says, "Those from among you shall build the old waste places; you shall raise up the foundations of many generations; and you shall be called the Repairer of the Breach; the Restorer of Streets to Dwell In" (Isa. 58:12). Once you are free, God can use you like a well-lit street to lead others to Him. He can use you like a bridge to reach those who are distant from Him. Through you He can take those lives that have been desolate and destroyed by addictions, oppression, and abuse and turn what was once a wasteland into a fruitful garden.

A friend of mine started a church in a barn many years ago. The interesting thing is, this barn was used as a dance hall all week long. But it wasn't used at all on Sunday mornings. My friend had very little money, but he managed to rent this barn for Sunday mornings at a very good price. There was just enough room for a little pulpit and some chairs for the congregation on the dance floor. He would go over there early on Sunday morning and get things cleaned up and set up. Little by little, people started to get saved. As the local people started to give their lives to the Lord, they stopped partying, and the barn and dance hall started losing money. Eventually they closed down completely, and my friend was able to buy the building. Years later he told me, "When we took this piece of property it was just fifty acres of wasteland. But now we've got a fruitful orchard on it." That's what God can do with your marriage, with your family. It is time to fast and pray for them, and don't give up. There may be nothing you *can* do...but there is nothing He *cannot* do.

The Lord responds to your brokenness when you tell Him, "Lord, I give You my heart and soul; You are the only one I live for. With every breath I take, Lord, I want You to have Your way in me." And then let Him show Himself strong through your life.

Chapter 5

Snowflake in the Amazon

I never cease to be amazed by how God can connect people to accomplish His purposes. Through the power of the Holy Spirit, God gives men and women talents, gifts, discernment, and insight that—when brought together with what has been given to someone else—can change the world. I'm honored to have many connections like that in my life. One such friend and partner in the faith is Dr. Bruce Wilkinson, author of the best-selling book *The Prayer of Jabez*. Bruce has preached at Free Chapel a couple of times, and on a recent visit I talked him into staying to record the *Kingdom Connection* broadcast with me. That was a powerful day! The Holy Spirit used my time with Bruce, while we were taping, to confirm and solidify something that had been stirring in my spirit for a long time: taking the gospel to the nations.

There is something in each of us that desires more. When we choose to submit those desires to God, He can do great things with us. Fasting helps you bring your desires into alignment with God's desires. I don't believe we were made to merely float along in a mediocre Christian life. God never intended us to be selfish and say, "Well, I have enough." That is what first intrigued me about Jabez when I first began to study his story over twenty years ago. Jabez makes a brief appearance in just two verses:

> Now Jabez was more honorable than his brothers, and his mother called his name Jabez, saying, "Because I bore him in pain." And Jabez called on the God of Israel saying, "Oh, that You would bless me indeed, and enlarge my territory, that Your hand would be with me, and that You would keep me from evil, that I may not cause pain!" So God granted him what he requested.
>
> —1 Chronicles 4:9–10

He was an honorable man, and God granted his request. I was glad when Bruce's book came out because it broadened my understanding so much more. The Lord led him on a journey to discover the power of the prayer Jabez prayed in those verses and how that same prayer is so closely related to the Great Commission today. As Bruce shared during our conversation, "The last thing Jesus talked about when He was on this earth was to make it clear that He wanted us to enlarge our territory to include the whole world." In Acts chapter 1, before Jesus ascended to heaven, He told those gathered around Him, "But you shall receive power when the Holy Spirit has come upon you; and you shall be witnesses to Me in Jerusalem, and in all Judea and Samaria, and to the end of the earth" (v. 8). Talk about enlarging your territory!

There was a time when Free Chapel reached a place of decision. We had completed a large, beautiful campus where more than thirty-three hundred people could worship God freely in the main sanctuary, members could fellowship and have a meal together, and their children could be challenged and taught in a safe, state-of-the-art facility. Our broadcasts were reaching millions, and we were doing a lot around the world. It was all paid for. We were debt free. We had arrived at that place where we could have honestly just kicked back and enjoyed the blessings God had poured out on us. But I felt the prompting of the Holy Spirit saying, "There's more." We are never to settle for that mediocre, lukewarm spirit. If you're not careful, it can creep into your walk with God. You start to think, "I'm saved. I'm on my way to heaven. I'm good. I've got all of God that I need." I want to assure you: that is wrong thinking. You have much more room to be enlarged in your spirit and in the dream God has for your life. Where there is no hope in the future, there is no power in the present.

Jabez didn't pray, "Oh, that You would bless me indeed so I could enjoy it all for myself and not care who else is in need." I believe that the Holy Spirit has a plan to get you to the places and the people that He wants to connect with you. When you ask God to enlarge your territory, what you are really saying is, "Lord, thank You for the achievements of the past, but don't let it stop; I believe there is more that I can do." I love Caleb's attitude. That man was eighty-five years old when he went to Joshua and asked for the mountain that Moses had promised him as his inheritance. It was the land he and the others were sent to spy out. Caleb and Joshua came back with the good report that they could take the land—but the other spies turned the hearts of the people against it. Caleb and Joshua had to wander in that desert with the rest of the Israelites for the next forty years, *without* murmuring or complaining. Then Caleb approached Joshua and said:

> As yet I am as strong this day as on the day that Moses sent me; just as my strength was then, so now is my strength for war, both for going out and for coming in. Now therefore, give me this mountain of which the LORD spoke in that day; for you heard in that day how the Anakim were there, and that the cities were great and fortified. It may be that the LORD will be with me, and I shall be able to drive them out as the LORD said.
>
> —JOSHUA 14:11–12

Caleb was set. He was going to be taken care of. The children of Israel had come into the Promised Land. But Caleb knew *there was more*. For forty years he kept his mouth shut and settled for "mediocre," even though he could have been in the Promised Land all that time if the rest of the people had trusted God rather than believing a negative report. He believed there were more great battles to fight as long as the Lord would be with him. If the Lord said Caleb could drive out the giants in that land when he was forty, then Caleb—even at eighty-five—was willing to say, "Here I am, Lord; expand my territory for Your glory!"

Caleb was one old man who dared to believe God for mighty things. In Joshua chapter 15 we see that Caleb successfully took the mountain, driving out the giants in the land just as God has promised. His persistence was passed on to the next generation too. After he conquered Hebron, Caleb's daughter, who had been promised in marriage to the man who helped him also take the land of Kirjath Sepher, asked to enlarge her territory. She said to her father, "Give me a blessing; since you have given me land in the South, give me also springs of water." So he gave her the upper springs and the lower springs" (Josh. 15:19).

The "If My People" Fast...

Jabez was one little man. One person. One honorable man whose prayer God answered. In 2 Chronicles 7:14, a verse many are familiar with, God says, "If My *people*..." Do you know what it takes to be God's people? You have to first be God's *person*. God's one little man or woman. God's teenager. God's aging warrior. God's Jabez who caused his mama pain at birth, or Caleb who will say with a humble, passionate heart, "God, I want more. I want more of You, and I want to do more for You." For that kind of person there are great rewards and promises to be discovered in the "if...thens" of God's Word. The full verse reads:

> If My people who are called by My name will humble themselves, and pray and seek My face, and turn from their wicked ways, then I will hear from heaven, and will forgive their sin and heal their land.
>
> —2 Chronicles 7:14

First, in order to be the people of God, you must be a person of God. The next thing God requires in this promise is *humility*. What does it mean to humble yourself? There are dozens of DIY (do it yourself) shows on TV these days, even an entire DIY Network on cable. Shows with names like *I Hate My Kitchen*, *Renovation Realities*, and *Yard Crashers* feature loads of advice on how to tear down and rebuild your kitchen, your house, and your yard with your own two hands and a few tools.

> When you ask God to enlarge your territory, what you are really saying is, "Lord, thank You for the achievements of the past, but don't let it stop; I believe there is more that I can do."

When it comes to humbling yourself, the DIY show would be called *Pride Crashers*, and the main tool utilized would be fasting!

Fasting is self-humbling. David prayed, "But as for me, when they were sick, my clothing was sackcloth; *I humbled myself with fasting*" (Ps. 35:13, emphasis added). Ezra needed to cross a dangerous territory with a large group of people and little children. So he said, "I proclaimed a fast there at the river of Ahava, *that we might humble ourselves* before our God, to seek from Him the right way for us and our little ones and all our possessions" (Ezra 8:21, emphasis added). Ezra "leaned not on his own understanding" but humbled himself and asked God to show him the best way to travel.[1] The disciples were squabbling about rank and superiority when Jesus told them, "Assuredly, I say to you, unless you are converted and become as little children, you will by no means enter the kingdom of heaven. Therefore whoever humbles himself as this little

child is the greatest in the kingdom of heaven" (Matt. 18:
3–4). Later, as we see in Matthew 23, Jesus told His disciples and the multitudes that were gathered, "Whoever
exalts himself [with haughtiness and empty pride] shall
be humbled (brought low), and whoever humbles himself
[whoever has a modest opinion of himself and behaves
accordingly] shall be raised to honor" (v. 12, AMP).

In the last chapter I covered how God rebuked the
people of Isaiah's day who were fasting out of religious
routine. They were actually taking *pride* in their faithfulness to fast. Jesus shared a similar parable of the Pharisee
and the tax collector.

> Also He spoke this parable to some who trusted
> in themselves that they were righteous, and
> despised others: "Two men went up to the
> temple to pray, one a Pharisee and the other a
> tax collector. The Pharisee stood and prayed thus
> with himself, 'God, I thank You that I am not
> like other men—extortioners, unjust, adulterers,
> or even as this tax collector. I fast twice a week;
> I give tithes of all that I possess.' And the tax
> collector, standing afar off, would not so much
> as raise his eyes to heaven, but beat his breast,
> saying, 'God, be merciful to me a sinner!' I tell
> you, this man went down to his house justified
> rather than the other; for everyone who exalts

himself will be humbled, and he who humbles himself will be exalted."

—Luke 18:9–14

Jesus shared this with people who He knew "trusted in themselves," considering themselves righteous and despising everyone else. They would have starred on the first episode of *Pride Crashers*! The Pharisee was fasting, but he was fasting without humility. It was just another pompous, religious routine. Fasting is humbling yourself, a command repeated over and over in the Scriptures. I believe in this powerful promise from God. Fasting as a means of humbling ourselves is clearly a prerequisite to the rest.

Once we as God's people begin to humble ourselves through fasting, He invites us to pray and seek His face. Second Chronicles 7:14 in the Amplified version reads, "...shall humble themselves, pray, seek, crave, and require of necessity My face." Fasting, I believe, is our way of stepping into the heart of God that grieves for hurting, broken humanity that He created and loves. Fasting embraces emptiness and starves haughtiness. It is a form of withdrawing from normal life in the regular world that we live in, emptying ourselves of not just food but anything else that we "seek, crave, and require of necessity" other than His face. We should fast not just food but also entertainment, media, and worldly junk—delicacies from the world's table—things that contaminate and limit the power of a fast. Fasting is our "body language" to God. When we fast, we are expressing our heart hunger for Jesus and how serious we are about hearing His voice and following His ways. From a place of humbleness when we pray and seek His face, we get His eyes, His ears, and His voice. We position ourselves to be "lifted up" to see how He sees, to hear what He wants us to hear, and to learn the sound of His whisper guiding our steps. When we pray and seek Him instead of just what He can do for us, we are compelled to proceed to the next step: turning from wicked ways.

There comes a point in your life when you have to *turn*. No more compromise. No more double life. No more hidden sins that are only hidden in your mind—God sees them, and most of the people close to you probably do as well. It is time to make the choice that anything in your life that does not line up with the Word of God has to go. When you set your heart to fast and seek God's face, humbling yourself before Him, He will be faithful to show you those areas in your life that eat away like a cancer at your soul and keep you from entering the fullness that He has for you. Fasting and praying make you much more aware of His tremendous grace and mercy that are available to you—to break every chain of the devil!

Wickedness is not just limited to immoral living, sinful habits, and iniquities. The Bible says wickedness is even manifested in unforgiveness and when you bury your talent. In Matthew 18 Jesus told the parable of the servant who owed ten thousand talents but was unable to pay. He was to be sold, and his family with him, to repay the debt. But he pleaded for mercy and was forgiven all his debt out of the compassion of the master. That same servant went out and immediately started beating up another servant who owed him a much smaller debt—and had him thrown in prison over it! When the compassionate master heard about it, he became enraged and said, "You wicked servant! I forgave you all that debt because you begged me. Should you not also have had compassion on your fellow servant, just as I had pity on you?" (vv. 32–33). Jesus concluded this parable with the warning, "So My heavenly Father also will do to you if each of you, from his heart, does not forgive his brother his trespasses" (v. 35).

A parable is a story with a lesson that is intended for its hearers to apply to their lives. In Matthew 25 Jesus told another parable about a man leaving for a journey. The man had servants, "and to one he gave five talents, to another two, and to another one, to each according to his own ability" (v. 15). The man who received one talent had ability. He may not have had the same ability as the other two, but he did have the ability to do something with the talent he was given. But he didn't—he buried it instead. The other two presented their master with an increase when he returned, but not this guy. He just dug

"Then I Will Hear From Heaven..."

When we seriously commit to humble ourselves, pray, and seek God's face and turn from wickedness, He promises to hear us! He promises to forgive our sin and heal our land. Our land—this nation—is in deep need of healing. One person alone cannot stop the sin of abortion in our land, but God can when we humble ourselves and seek Him. One person alone cannot stop the tide of immorality sweeping America, but God can forgive our sin and heal our land. If He raised His hand to blot out wickedness in the land today—how many believers who haven't forgiven someone, who haven't used what God gave them, who haven't broken the hold of past sinful habits and iniquities would get swept away with the rest?

This promise is for all of us, every day: if we will—He will. When you fast and pray in this way, it will affect generations! When you lay a solid foundation of humbling yourself in fasting and in prayer and in turning from wickedness, the impact will be immeasurable. Most people have never heard of a man named George McCluskey. But George was a praying man. I don't know for certain if he mixed fasting with his praying, but I believe he did. George was concerned about his children and decided to set aside one hour each day to pray for them. Every single day from 11:00 a.m. to noon, he prayed for his children. His two daughters eventually married ministers, and his son became a minister. Their children grew up and married or became ministers. And one of George's granddaughters just happened to become the mother of someone most people have heard of: Dr. James Dobson, founder of Focus on the Family and now *Family Talk*. Dr. Dobson shared on a radio program recently that his great-grandfather's daily prayer time was somewhat legendary in the family. George McCluskey passed away a short time before James Dobson was born. But his prayers, stored up on James's behalf, have helped to bless and keep him. Dobson said his great-grandfather got it wrong in one area though. It seems that George announced to the family before he died that the Lord promised him that every member of their family for four generations would be in ministry. But the promise has extended even beyond that to the fifth generation, with Dobson's son, Ryan, serving the Lord as an ordained minister.[2]

Let the River Flow!

I believe God is ready to release a mighty river of His presence and power in our land, but I don't think it will come in a sudden wave. I believe He is waiting for the "persons" of God to unite in fasting, praying, and seeking His face. Because for God, one person becomes like that one uniquely crafted snowflake that quietly lands on the peak of the Andes Mountain range. When the temperatures rise, those individual flakes melt, forming tiny rivulets. Those tiny rivulets merge together to feed small streams. Those small streams feed larger streams, and those larger streams flow into the largest river in the world—the mighty Amazon River. The Amazon didn't start as the largest river in the world…it started as one snowflake. Yet it releases the largest volume of water into the ocean of any other river on earth. The force and volume of the Amazon is so strong that its freshwater flow pushes back the salty ocean waters of the Atlantic for about 250 miles! It is said to even change the color of the Atlantic Ocean water in an area covering nearly 1 million square miles.[3] That gives a new perspective to Habakkuk's words, "For the earth will be filled with the knowledge of the glory of the LORD, as the waters cover the sea" (Hab. 2:14).

> When you lay a solid foundation of humbling yourself in fasting and in prayer and in turning from wickedness, the impact will be immeasurable.

Clearly, it is time we regained the edge! God is looking for a person, for people, who will fast and pray, seek His face, and turn from wickedness. Those people will form a mighty river that will push back darkness and uncleanness.

It will break lose the chains of bondage and set free the bound. When our bellies are emptied of the junk of the world, then, as Jesus said, a holy river of living water will flow![4]

It is time to stop waiting on someone else to do it. God said, "If My people." Not the world. Not the Democrats. Not the Republicans. Jesus said, "My sheep [my people] hear my voice, and I know them, and they follow Me" (John 10:27). It is time we get serious and truly follow Jesus in His example. Before doing any ministry—He fasted, sharpening His ax for the battles ahead. Jesus said, "And whoever exalts himself will be humbled, and he who humbles himself will be exalted" (Matt. 23:12). Man cannot hold you down when God exalts you. Your influence for God will spread like that forceful Amazon and push back the darkness. The system cannot keep you back. The people can't hinder you when God says, "I will exalt."

The context of this promise found in 2 Chronicles 7:14 is the completion of the temple. Solomon had finished building the house of God and had an elaborate celebration to dedicate it to the Lord. God was pleased, choosing it for Himself as a place of sacrifice. We often overlook the verses before and after verse 14. God said when difficult times come, even from His hand, if His people humble themselves and pray, seek His face, and turn from wickedness, then He will forgive and heal the damage our sin has brought upon the land. He promised that His eye would be upon that place, that church, that people, that person who does this.

It is time that we pray and seek God's face and turn from wickedness. It is time to stop complaining that there is not a voice in government that will speak against immorality, against the business of murdering unborn children, against human trafficking, against the homosexual agenda—and become that mighty river, the voice that God will use to flood a nation with righteousness, with His glory. I fly across this country each week in order to preach at both Free Chapel campuses. Sometimes on those trips my heart is so heavy for America. I believe God is able to intervene and make America great, greater than she's ever been. But we need to cry out for nationwide intervention! Asking God, as Jabez did, to expand your borders and bless you does not mean the manifestation of that prayer stops inside your front door. It's not about "us four and no more." This is about nationwide and worldwide intervention.

Bigger Baskets?

I preached on the life and the prayer of Jabez one Sunday morning in 2003 at Free Chapel. We were still in our former building on McEver Road at the time. The Lord had impressed me strongly to tell the congregation to "get bigger baskets," because He was about to enlarge our borders. It was just a little word from God. A simple, rhema word that inspired the congregation to fast and pray into what God was calling us to do. We took it seriously.

Jabez prayed, "Bless me indeed, and enlarge my territory." But there are some requirements for anyone desiring to have their territory enlarged. I have found some specific requirements related to this in the fifty-fourth chapter of Isaiah. The chapter starts out encouraging the barren to sing because things are about to change and get stretched all over the place. Barrenness is to be unfulfilled. But barrenness does not intimidate God. The solution to barrenness requires enlarging and stretching.

> Enlarge the place of your tent,
> And let them stretch out the curtains of your
>   dwellings;
> Do not spare;
> Lengthen your cords,
> And strengthen your stakes.
>
> —ISAIAH 54:2

First, we must reject smallness. Enlargement requires us to get out of our small boxes, our small routines, our small thinking, and our limited view of God. We think way too small for God's economy and ability. We need to advance and not shrink back, always thankful, but always believing God for more. Caleb and Joshua saw a place of enlargement before them, but the rest shrunk back and stayed small. Caleb and Joshua believed it could be done, but the rest said they were afraid to try and remained small-minded. When you get God's vision for enlarging your tent, you get tired of talking about small stuff all the time. You get fed up with hearing what can't be done. If you wait until everything is perfect before you step out and follow the Lord, you will never do anything. If you let small things trip you up and occupy your time, smallness will take over your life and rob you of what God wants to do in your life.

Second, enlarging the place of your tent means making room for some new people in your life. People will s-t-r-e-t-c-h you! Prepare to get some stretch marks; they are a sign that your barrenness has come to an end. Relationships with people will stretch your nerves, stretch your patience, and stretch your prayer life. A rubber band will never fulfill its purpose until it is stretched—and neither will you and I. When we are stretched, that is when we are most vulnerable. That is what we do not like about stretching. We want to be comfortable and safe. It is easier to sit on our blessed assurance and just wait for the Rapture to come rather than to believe God for greater things. But if you want more, if you're tired of an unfulfilled, unfruitful, barren life, then God is saying, "Enlarge and stretch." You will never see a miracle until you stretch your faith. The Lord stretched us from our Brown's Bridge location over to the McEver Road facility, and then He stretched us to this 150-acre campus. But He didn't stop there. Now we are stretching this current building to facilitate about two thousand more of our friends and family in this area that we are praying for—praying for them to be saved and set free.

Now, something has to support all the expanding and stretching. I believe that is why the prophet said, "Do not spare." If you are going to be enlarged and stretched, it will require some new, longer cords to hold that tent up, and you have to drive some strong stakes down deep into the ground to keep the proper tension on those cords.

I'll never forget the first and only camping trip my family ever embarked upon. The kids were still very young at the time. Someone loaned us a big tent, so we made plans to leave our comfortable house right after church one Sunday and drive up to the mountains to have a wonderful time camping with the children. Of course, we got a late start, so we didn't arrive at the campsite until it was almost dark. Using the headlights on the car, I began trying to pitch the big tent. By then, all the babies were crying and hungry. I frantically tied the tent cords to all kinds of things just to try and get it to look right and be secure. I finally got it looking somewhat correct, and we got all the children fed and settled. It was going pretty well until sometime in the middle of the night when my wife said, "Something is dripping on my head." It had started to rain. Worse yet, it had started to rain *inside* the tent. I turned on the flashlight to discover that the entire top of the tent had caved in! I had not used long enough cords or strong enough stakes—a painful lesson to learn when your wife is getting rained on in the middle of the night. We hurried out of the tent, packed up the car, and drove to the nearest hotel, leaving that whole experience far behind us.

When God tells you to lengthen your cords, it means lengthen your reach. Wider tents require longer cords to keep them securely held in place. Once you lengthen your cords, you must also strengthen your stakes. Don't tie your tent to flimsy tree branches if you want it to hold. You have to drive big, strong stakes deep into the ground. With increased extension you must have increased stability. Calamity strikes when you are growing outwardly without increasing your stability and driving your stakes deeper into the bedrock of God's truth. Life is like a huge tree. An increase in the branches requires an increase in the roots. The more the branches spread, the deeper the roots must grow.

I remember preaching that Sunday morning on the prayer of Jabez and saying that God was going to expand this ministry from east to west and internationally. We didn't have a campus in California at that time, but soon after, the Lord spoke to me during a fast that the doors were opening for us to expand to the west. Our international broadcasts continue to expand and reach more souls for Jesus. I believe these expansions and solid growth are born in faithfulness to fast. There is both reward and wisdom to be found when we tune out the noise of the world and come away to hear God's heart through fasting and prayer. That is when you can hear that simple word that can take you from glory unto glory, from faith unto faith, from building unto building, from nation unto nation, from multitudes to more multitudes of souls. Every time this ministry has gone from one level to another, God has done it. But God had to take us as a people and put us through the expanding and the stretching, the lengthening and the strengthening. We felt the pressure and the stress of it, but I am so glad we did not spare; we did not draw back.

Chapter 6

Hunger Meets Hunger

Most of us have no problem figuring out when it is time to eat. As a general rule, we were all raised having breakfast in the morning, lunch midday, and dinner in the evening. I remember some farming families "in the old days" that would have huge breakfasts before the sun came up so they could go out and start their day at sunrise on a full stomach. Others would get up before daylight and work for several hours in the cool of the day before coming in for breakfast, and then they wouldn't eat the evening meal until very late in the evening. There are fad diets today that tell us to eat six or seven small meals throughout the day rather than just three main meals. Newborn babies may require feeding every couple of hours for the first few weeks. Ultimately, we eat when we get hungry!

But how do you know when to fast? I mean, it's easy to recognize physical hunger, but what about spiritual hunger? There are times when your church may call for a corporate fast, inviting all who are part of that body of believers to rally together and participate for a specific cause. We receive calls, letters, and e-mails from around the world from churches that have joined the fasting movement, participating in the first of the year twenty-one-day fast, and they are reaping the rewards of their faithfulness. But there are also times when you should fast on your own, and you need to know how to recognize those times.

Mammoth Tasks

Have you ever been faced with something that you knew was impossible to accomplish on your own? Nearly 150 years after the Assyrians conquered the northern tribes of Israel and the Babylonian armies took the tribes of Judah captive, the city of Jerusalem sat in ruins. The temple was destroyed, the wall was broken down, and the gates were burned down. Only a few families remained, and they just moved around the piles of rubble. A man named Nehemiah worked in the palace of the king of Shushan, about eight hundred miles from Jerusalem. God gave Nehemiah a burden for the city of his people. When he received word about the condition of Jerusalem, he said, "So it was, when I heard these words, that I sat down and wept, and mourned for many days; I was fasting and praying before the God of heaven" (Neh. 1:4). Nehemiah knew he had to do something. He fasted and prayed, interceding for the sins of the people of Israel and asking God to grant him favor with his boss, the king. God gave Nehemiah a dream to rebuild the walls. It was a mammoth task—and only God could make it happen.

The Book of Nehemiah is very encouraging! It is a good read when you are on a fast. When you think about it, Nehemiah was probably living pretty well in the king's employ. Yet he longed to let it all go in order to accomplish the assignment that God had put on his heart. Against amazing odds Nehemiah got the job done! He wrote in his journal, "So the wall was finished on the twenty-fifth day of Elul, *in fifty-two days*. And it happened, when all our enemies heard of it, and all the nations around us saw these things, that they were very disheartened in their own eyes; for they perceived that this work was done by our God" (Neh. 6:15–16, emphasis added). God not only made a way for him to do it, but He also empowered and equipped Nehemiah to do it in a ridiculously short period of time. Nehemiah sharpened his ax before he began! He sliced through the constant threats of the enemy and got the job done.

You may not be rebuilding city walls, but God has put a dream in your heart. Fast and pray for His means and direction to accomplish it. Perhaps you are starting a new business, a new ministry, a new career, or a new family.

Maybe you have decided to adopt a troubled child or one suffering from physical disabilities. Fast and pray for God's power and direction to accomplish the task.

Physical Danger or Under Attack

Queen Esther and all the Jews were under threat of extermination at the hand of Haman. He had manipulated the king in order to draft a decree calling for the Jews to be wiped off the face of the earth. Esther, though she was only a young girl, had learned a lot from her cousin Mordecai. She called a three-day fast for the Jews and even the people under her charge in the palace.[1] What the enemy intended for evil, God turned around for good because someone humbled themselves, fasted and prayed, and sought His face! Haman and all his sons were hanged on the gallows intended for Mordecai, and the Jews were spared.[2]

In 2 Chronicles chapter 20, Jehoshaphat was surrounded by his enemies.

> It happened after this that the people of Moab with the people of Ammon, and others with them besides the Ammonites, came to battle against Jehoshaphat. Then some came and told Jehoshaphat, saying, "A great multitude is coming against you from beyond the sea, from Syria; and

they are in Hazazon Tamar" (which is En Gedi). And Jehoshaphat feared, and set himself to seek the Lord, and proclaimed a fast throughout all Judah. So Judah gathered together to ask help from the Lord; and from all the cities of Judah they came to seek the Lord.

—2 Chronicles 20:1–4

Jehoshaphat called a corporate fast, and the people were highly motivated to join him in seeking the Lord! When they humbled themselves through fasting and seeking the Lord, they opened the door for God to not just deliver them but also to fight the battle *for* them. God answered Jehoshaphat's request, saying, "Do not be afraid nor dismayed because of this great multitude, for the battle is not yours, but God's" (v. 15).

Are you under attack? Is someone slandering you or threatening physical harm? It is time to fast and pray. Sometimes it feels like the enemy has come in like a flood against you—fast and pray. Are you facing something that will put you in physical danger? Are you facing surgery, a dangerous journey of some sort? Do you serve in the military or have a spouse, a son, or a daughter serving who is in physical danger? You should fast and pray. You can fast and pray for the protection of your children, just like Ezra who called for a fast to protect and lead "the little ones."

Appalled

When it comes to praying for the little ones, I don't know of a time in history when that was more necessary than today. The fact that we live in a society where human trafficking—specifically the sale of little children in the sex trade—could become the second highest crime in the nation is utterly appalling. Not simply because there are evil men and women who kidnap or otherwise coerce children into sex slavery—but because there are men who will pay to have sex with little children! The only thing more appalling is how long this nation has said that our children are disposable, beginning in the womb. When a child can be killed in the womb, what value will a nation place on a child once it is born? When our government discusses laws that will use your tax dollars to fund the murder of the unborn through legal abortion, it is time to fast and pray over the blood-guilt of this nation from millions of aborted children. The unborn are the littlest ones among us—and the most vulnerable for destruction in the name of convenience.

Demonic Oppression

Jesus said there are times when nothing but fasting and prayer will drive out the source of demonic oppression in someone's life. The disciples encountered this truth when they tried to cast a deaf and dumb spirit out of a man's son. When Jesus arrived:

> He rebuked the unclean spirit, saying to it, "Deaf and dumb spirit, I command you, come out of him and enter him no more!" Then the spirit cried out, convulsed him greatly, and came out of him....His disciples asked Him privately, "Why could we not cast it out?" So He said to them, "This kind can come out by nothing but prayer and fasting."
>
> —MARK 9:25–29

Demons are real, and demonic oppression is real. Jesus began His earthly ministry with a grueling forty-day fast and gave His followers authority over the power of the enemy.[3] The disciples had not been fasting while Jesus was with them, but it was clear they were expected to do so after He left.[4] People all over the world are bound by demonic oppression. God's "chosen fast" is for us, His people who are called by His name, to set free those who are bound and oppressed.

The Holy Spirit's Prompting

As I said before, the Holy Spirit knows when you need to fast. He led Jesus on His first fast in the wilderness. The

Holy Spirit knows when you are losing the edge in your life, when you are drifting and growing dull. He knows long before there is enough evidence for you to recognize it in your own life. Do not pass off His promptings to fast when things are "good." Jesus said of the Holy Spirit, "When He, the Spirit of truth, has come, He will guide you into all truth; for He will not speak on His own authority, but whatever He hears He will speak; and He will tell you things to come. He will glorify Me, for He will take of what is Mine and declare it to you. All things that the Father has are Mine. Therefore I said that He will take of Mine and declare it to you" (John 16:13–15). Twice Jesus said the Spirit of truth, the Comforter, would take what was His and make it known to us. The more you choose to make fasting and prayer part of your life, the more sensitive you become to the Spirit of God to know when it is time to fast.

> You can fast and pray for the protection of your children, just like Ezra who called for a fast to protect and lead "the little ones."

Your spirit hungers for the things of God just as your stomach hungers for food. In Samaria, the disciples brought lunch back for Jesus, but He told them He had food to eat that they knew nothing about—to do the will of the Father.[5] When you engage in seasons of fasting and prayer, you will experience a physical hunger, but it typically fades. More importantly, your spiritual hunger rises up and can only be satisfied with the will of God and fulfilling His calling on your life. People in Samaria were hungry for truth. The woman at the well came for well water, but Jesus knew her greater thirst would only be satisfied with Living Water. She left her pitcher behind and went away filled to overflowing. The disciples were concerned about filling their own bellies while Jesus was concerned about filling an entire city with the Bread of Life! Fasting as the Holy Spirit leads will help you come into alignment with the things God desires to do you in your life—for you and through you!

No Expiration Date

Sometimes you can pray for something, but you don't see the answer right away. Keep praying. Don't let go of your faith, and do not cast aside your confidence! It may be that the thing you are praying for is just not ready or in God's timing yet. Your prayers will not be ignored or discarded. Prayers don't have an expiration date! The Book of Revelation even refers to bowls of incense collected in heaven that are the prayers of the saints.[6] Daniel had been fasting and praying for three weeks when the angel of the

Lord appeared to him, explaining how his prayers had been heard in heaven since the first day, but the answer had been delayed:

> Then he said to me, "Do not fear, Daniel, for from the first day that you set your heart to understand, and to humble yourself before your God, your words were heard; and I have come because of your words. But the prince of the kingdom of Persia withstood me twenty-one days; and behold, Michael, one of the chief princes, came to help me, for I had been left alone there with the kings of Persia. Now I have come to make you understand what will happen to your people in the latter days, for the vision refers to many days yet to come."
>
> —DANIEL 10:12–14

When you pray in alignment with God's will, He hears. You can rest assured that you have set something in motion in the supernatural even if you are not able to discern them in the natural.

Acts chapter 10 is one of the most powerful chapters in the Bible. Prior to the events detailed in that chapter, only the Jews had received the good news of the gospel and the baptism of the Holy Spirit. But everything changed when one man's hunger and persistence penetrated heaven. Peter went up on the roof of his friend Simon's house to pray. He was hungry because it was lunchtime. But once again, when man was thinking about sinking his teeth into a big, juicy, well-done kosher steak, God had a far different plan for lunch!

One day earlier, an angel visited a devout Italian man who loved God. The man's prayers and giving had come up as a memorial before God. He was a Gentile, but he and his household believed in God and wanted to know Him. At the end of four days of prayer, and perhaps even fasting, the angel of the Lord appeared to this man named Cornelius and told him to send for a man named Peter. Cornelius's men headed out and arrived the next day while Peter was on the roof—receiving a vision about food of all things! God was using food to show Peter that He desired to pour out His Spirit on *all* flesh, including the Gentiles. The Gentiles included every one who was not of Jewish descent and were long considered by Jewish law to be unclean.

Two men, miles apart, became connected by hunger. Cornelius was praying with a hunger for God. Peter was on a roof at lunchtime receiving a message from God about food instead of chowing down on lunch. The two men were from opposite ends of the spectrum. One was a fisherman; the other was a soldier. One was a Jew; the other was a Gentile. They were total strangers, unknown to each other, but known by the Spirit of God. And by the Spirit of God, they were connected before they ever came face-to-face. Because of Cornelius's passion and hunger for God, a messenger was sent with specific instructions about Peter and where to find him! Imagine fasting and praying to the point that God sends an angel with specific instructions that lead to the release of captives and freedom to the oppressed.

One man was seeking; one man had the answer. Both men were praying, and a connection was made. Before they ever met physically, their prayers met in heaven. I think that is so powerful! Cornelius was storing up prayer in heaven. The next day (no expiration date on prayer) the Spirit of the Lord prepared Peter for his role in what had already been decreed in heaven. When Peter went up on that roof to pray at lunchtime, God made the prayer connection, opening the door of salvation to the Gentiles.

Making a Prayer Connection

I want you to understand that heaven has kingdom connections for you. When you pray, your prayers plug into God's connection of plans, resources, and power in heaven. All over this world there are connections that God is setting up—things we have no idea about, but by simply following the prompting of the Holy Spirit's call to fast, we take part in divinely orchestrated connections. It saddens me to think of how many people do not fast and therefore do not make these connections. Mordecai told his cousin, Esther, that someone else would be raised up if she didn't do what she needed to do. Why would you want to let your connection be made by someone else?

God heard the cry of the people of Israel when they were in slavery and oppressed in Egypt. He pulled Moses aside, interrupted his routine, and raised him up as a deliverer for Israel. All over the world today God hears the cries of the unsaved, the cries of the abused, the oppressed, the captive, those who follow false gods. He hears the six-year-old girl who cries out to a God she doesn't know, praying that her daddy will not sneak into her bed again that night and hurt her. He hears the sigh of the child who was sold into prostitution at fourteen years of age, who now at age eighteen has become hardened to the core in order to survive another day. He hears the alcoholic stumble home once again and the drug addict desperate to score another hit. He hears when one of them whispers, "God, if You're out there, please help me..." as they slip off into a chemical-induced haze. But here's the deal: there needs to be a prayer connection! Will you give up lunch once in a while to be that prayer connection? Jesus did. Peter did. Many others have and do.

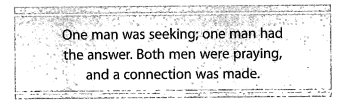

One man was seeking; one man had the answer. Both men were praying, and a connection was made.

Heed the Spirit's leading to fast from food and entertainment once in a while in order to dine instead on doing the will of God and seeing His work finished in someone else's life.

Cornelius was hungry for God to touch His family. He was praying for his household. He was praying for his children. But the connection for the Gentiles had not yet been made. Jesus came to seek and save the lost sheep of Israel first, and from Israel the rest of the world was to be reached.[7] Cornelius had not had a born-again salvation experience, but he was hungry for God, and his hunger met Peter's hunger in God's timing.

Each year when we start our twenty-one-day fast at Free Chapel, I pray that God will link our physical hunger to the spiritual hunger of drug addicts, alcoholics, the brokenhearted, the down-and-out as well as the up-and-in millionaire who has everything but Jesus.

Stacking Up Prayers

Notice that Cornelius's prayers "sizzled" in heaven for a while before the connection came to pass. In fact, the angel even told him that his prayers and generosity had come up as a memorial before God. Several years ago the Holy Spirit put it on my heart to pray for my children, because He would bring the right connections into their lives. At the time they were very little, so it was obvious that He wasn't going to bring their spouses along that day. But I understood that I would be "stacking up prayers" on their behalf, prayers He would use to make the right connections in their lives as they grew up: the right friends, the right opportunities, the right spouses, and so on. If you have children, I encourage you to do as George McCluskey did and start fasting and praying for your children to be born again, to meet the right friends, and to marry the right spouse. Stacking prayers in heaven led to five generations of his family all serving the Lord. Do you have lost loved ones? Sharpen your ax and start stacking up prayer! Before I met my wife I prayed and fasted that God would bring me the right spouse. I stacked up prayer that made a connection in heaven before I ever laid eyes on her on Earth. I was preaching the first time I saw her, and that is when God made the connection come full circle! Why would you want to connect on the Internet before you connect in heaven? I'm not saying that there is necessarily anything wrong with dating services, but dating services cannot do for you what the Holy Spirit can. Pray and fast! Your heavenly Father knows what you need and is able to make the right connections at the right time.

Connecting to Your Assignment

There is another way that fasting and praying make an important prayer connection in your life—to God's assignment. I know this personally because I was on a fast when the Lord made my assignment clear, calling me to preach. Up to that point I was seriously considering a career in music. In the nearly twenty-five years since that time, He has continued to give me specific "alignment for assignments" during a fast. Many developments in my life and ministry since then have been made clear as I have continued to fast and pray, seeking God's direction. Peter and Cornelius made a prayer connection, and both discovered God's assignment. Peter was to break the long-held divide between Jew and Gentile by sharing what God had given him with Cornelius and his family. But it didn't end there. Another connection was coming that would give us nearly half of the books of the New Testament. Fasting puts you in alignment for your assignment.

A young man named Saul watched as Stephen, a follower of Jesus who was full of the Holy Spirit, was dragged from the synagogue and brutally stoned to death outside of the city. As a young Hebrew devoted to the Law, this incident fueled Saul's desire to stamp out the dangerous "sect" that followed Jesus even after His death. Acts 8:3 reads, "As for Saul, he made havoc of the church, entering every house, and dragging off men and women, committing them to prison." On his way to the city of Damascus with permission from the high priest to arrest any followers he encountered, Saul's world was turned upside down. He found way more than he planned to on that trip when he met *the* High Priest! As the story continues in Acts 9, Saul was knocked to the ground and engulfed by a bright light. He heard the voice of a man speaking. When he humbly asked who was speaking to him, he heard, "I am Jesus, whom you are persecuting" (v. 5). At that moment Saul lost his sight and had to be led by his men the rest of the way to Damascus. He fasted there for three days, no doubt praying and pondering the unmistakable encounter he'd had on the road. But the Lord didn't leave him like that. He had a connection planned. Fasting got him in alignment for his assignment.

> Do you have lost loved ones? Sharpen your ax and start stacking up prayer!

Across town there lived a man named Ananias who was hungry for God and eager to serve. In a vision he received instructions to find Saul, who had already been told that Ananias would be coming. Ananias was instructed to lay hands on Saul's eyes so that he could receive his sight again. After that connection was made, Saul went immediately from persecuting Christians to becoming one, and went on preach the truth of God's Word to the Jews and especially to the Gentiles. After changing his name to Paul, he went from being full of religious zeal to being full of passion for Jesus. He wrote to his Hebrew brethren in Rome, "My heart's desire and prayer to God for Israel is that they may be saved. For I bear them witness that they have a zeal for God, but not according to knowledge. For they being ignorant of God's righteousness, and seeking to establish their own righteousness, have not submitted to the righteousness of God. For Christ is the end of the law for righteousness to everyone who believes" (Rom. 10:1–4).

Could there be other "Pauls" out there just waiting for God's connection to be made? Could you be the one God will use to drop the scales from their eyes? When you fast and pray, you connect with God's assignment for your life, those "good works" I mentioned before that God has prepared for us to walk in.[8] When you don't fast and pray, you do not connect with God's assignment. I love the fact that we get our assignment from God when we break out of the routine and seek Him in prayer and fasting. We can connect so God can direct our lives. It is time to quit worrying about everything and pray. When you pray, your prayer becomes the "plug" that plugs into God's resources.

Connecting to Your Community

Something else I love about these two stories is that neither Cornelius's men, nor Ananias had to travel far. Cornelius was in Caesarea, barely thirty miles from Joppa, where Peter was staying. Ananias lived in Damascus, so technically God brought Paul to him! I am always amazed when I hear someone say they are hesitant to pray for God's assignment because they don't want to be sent to a far-off land...as if God wouldn't make a way for that to work out. But most of the time there is someone right in your own neighborhood whom God wants to use you to touch! There may be someone right down the road who has been crying out saying, "God, if You're real...if You're out there..." His or her prayers may have been sizzling in heaven for weeks and months, waiting on one of God's children to be hungry enough to make the connection. The person may be at rock bottom because of a nasty divorce. He or she may be so destroyed by life that they are suicidal, just longing for someone to bring light to their darkness. They don't care about religion and church. They've been turned off by it all. Can you forgo a meal or two, seeking God on behalf of those in your own community to see that they receive the Bread of Life? When you fast, God will position you to be in the right place, at the right time, for the right blessing. I have seen truly gifted people struggle because they were in the wrong place, and

I have seen less talented people thrive because they found the right place. Location matters!

Maybe that prayer connection is waiting right inside your own home. Is there a spirit of division eroding the foundation of your marriage and your family? You need to fast and pray, breaking down strongholds and stacking up prayer for God to bring unity into your home. God is able to make the connection work even in your own family.

Persistence Breaks Resistance

One of the things the enemy hates most about fasting is persistence. That is why I love longer fasts like our annual twenty-one-day fast. When you make it through the first few days of his lies telling you that you can't make it—you get stronger and the resistance becomes weaker. When Jesus ended His forty-day fast, the Bible says the devil fled from Him. As you persist, before long it has been a week, then two weeks, then you are in the final stretch, and nothing can hold you back.

I believe that is how some of the miracles we read about in God's Word came about—through persistence. Think about the story of the woman who had been bleeding for years in Luke chapter 8. Doctors could do nothing to help her. She was considered "unclean" by the people of her time and basically ignored unless she came near a crowd, who would then move away from her for fear of contamination. But she heard about Jesus. Even though she was outcast, even if she had to crawl, she would not be denied the opportunity to touch at least the very edge of His garment. Who would know? And maybe, just maybe, her healing would come forth. So she pressed, she persisted, she made her way through the mob that surrounded Jesus that day, and with a shaking arm she reached her dirty fingers out to grasp the edge of His robe. She quickly let go, no doubt overwhelmed by the warmth of God's love that began to flow through her body and heal what was wrong with her. She felt the power of the Lord because of her persistence—and He felt her! He felt power leave Him and stopped everything to find out who it was. Luke wrote, "Now when the woman saw that she was not hidden, she came trembling; and falling down before Him, she declared to Him in the presence of all the people the reason she had touched Him and how she was healed immediately" (v. 47).

When you are praying and fasting, your persistence breaks resistance. It brings you to a place where you can feel God move powerfully in your life—but it also causes Him to feel your need, just as He felt the woman who needed healing touch Him in the midst of that huge crowd.[9] Fasting not only positions you to feel God—but it also positions you for Him to hear your heart's cry as well. Whatever forces have been resisting what God had coming in your life, your persistence will break resistance.

Start Stacking!

Regardless of whether you gave your life to Jesus eighty years ago or if you just got saved eight minutes ago, it is not too late to start stacking up prayers in heaven! Jesus taught a parable about a vineyard owner who needed help with the harvest. He hired guys first thing in the morning and promised them a denarius for a day's work. He went back several more times throughout the day and hired more men. At the last hour he found a few men who had been standing around all day because no one had hired them. He sent them to his field, where they worked only about an hour before the shift was over. He decided to be generous, so he paid the last men hired a denarius—just like the first who were hired and had worked all day. If your family is in shambles, I assure you that it is not too late for you to fast and pray to ask God to intervene! It is time to be persistent and break down the resistance.

If you are born again, have you ever asked who stacked up prayers for your salvation? I bet someone did. Maybe it was your great-great-grandmother. It could have been a spinster aunt who had no children of her own, so she stacked up prayers for her brother's and sister's children instead. Maybe it was a young man with a call of God on his life, fasting and praying for anyone in his school who didn't know Jesus. I've heard from our youth here at Free Chapel who do that. They join on the annual fast, and they stack up prayers for others. You'll know who it was once you get to heaven. For now, allow God to use you to make the connection for others. Let your hunger be stirred up to connect with their hunger. Fast, pray, cry out to God, and make someone else's name or situation come up to Him as a memorial.

Chapter 7

You Can't Do God's Will With Human Zeal

I have heard people say that they cannot afford to fast. Now, if there is a legitimate medical reason behind that claim, then absolutely under no circumstances should you attempt to fast. But I know a few guys who actually would have been fined thousands of dollars if they fasted. Free Chapel is home to a wide variety of people from all different backgrounds and professions. One year, as the time for our annual fast was drawing near, I was approached by a few of the Atlanta Falcon football players who are part of our Free Chapel congregation. They wanted to tell me that they were committing to fast and seek God for seven days. You need to understand that these are very, very big guys who would actually be penalized if they lost weight, regardless of the reason behind the loss. Choosing to fast presented a serious dilemma for them, but they were determined. They put their heads together and came up with a solution to be part of that powerful spiritual fast while maintaining their weight. They counted the cost and how much more effort it would take—and they plowed forward. That really touched my heart! It would have been so easy for them to just say that their job responsibilities prevented them from fasting. They are NFL football players, and their weight and physical condition are part of the price. But just as Daniel and his men were *healthier* after they fasted the goodies on the king's table, so were these guys. These physically powerful young men submitted themselves to God and found a way to make it work because they desired more of Him.

Who Is in Control?

It is so easy to come up with reasons not to fast, especially when it comes to jobs, sports, our overly worshiped entertainment, and, last but not least, convenience. Fasting breaks the routine, and that is *in*convenient. But like that old John Wayne movie, it takes "true grit" to submit yourself to God through fasting and prayer and to turn from the things of this world. Take a closer look at what James had to say about "humbling ourselves":

> Whoever therefore wants to be a friend of the world makes himself an enemy of God. Or do you think that the Scripture says in vain, "The Spirit who dwells in us yearns jealously"? But He

gives more grace. Therefore He says: "God resists the proud, but gives grace to the humble."

Therefore submit to God. Resist the devil and he will flee from you. Draw near to God and He will draw near to you. Cleanse your hands, you sinners; and purify your hearts, you double-minded. Lament and mourn and weep! Let your laughter be turned to mourning and your joy to gloom. Humble yourselves in the sight of the Lord, and He will lift you up.

—JAMES 4:4–10

That sounds very much like an invitation to fast! James makes it pretty clear that we can either submit to God or submit to the world. Likewise, we are either resisting the devil or resisting God. If we are not drawing closer to God, we are drifting farther from Him. Fasting is a choice to break the allure of the world and all its trappings as we put our flesh under submission. When you turn from the things of the world and submit yourself to God, He will give you the grace to stand strong and resist the temptations of the enemy. Especially on an extended fast, you will discover that time spent fasting, praying, and meditating on God's Word cleanses and purifies your heart and focuses your thoughts on things above rather than the stuff of this world.

Remember the days of Noah?[1] In that corrupt generation, he alone found favor in God's eyes. He was laboring away on the boat God told him to build while everyone else was laughing, drinking, eating, getting married, and just having a joyous time as they mocked the man of God. If it takes a flood to get your attention—it's too late! God calls us to be sober-minded, to get focused on His purposes, and to trust His grace. Fasting is not happy hour. Fasting is a time when you embrace emptiness. You become more and more sensitive to the Spirit of God, often to the point where weeping is the only expression of what is happening inside your heart.

It takes work to get your flesh under submission. Paul explained that the flesh wars against the Spirit—and the Spirit wars against the flesh.[2] So you need to ask yourself: Which one are you empowering? Which one are you giving access to control your life?

I go through all kinds of extremes during an extended fast. One thing I notice is mood swings. One minute I am eager and confident about the fast, and just a few hours later thoughts such as, "What's the use? This is crazy!", start filtering through my mind. After a few more days I move into "the grind" mode. Fasting *grinds* on your flesh. I will talk about this more later in the chapter. But as many times as I have fasted, it never fails that at some point on every fast I become overwhelmed with the feeling of uselessness. In fact, the enemy raises his ugly head to drive that point home as he whispers, "What good is it really doing? Give up." That is when I remind myself that I'm sharpening my ax, I'm regaining my edge, and I'm going to take him out! I think about how Satan came and sat with Jesus during His forty-day fast in the desert. He probably sat right in front of Jesus and ate a whole chocolate cake, followed by a big, juicy, perfectly grilled steak, and a steaming baked potato while tempting the Lord to quit that fast!

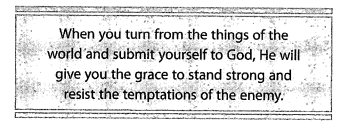

When you turn from the things of the world and submit yourself to God, He will give you the grace to stand strong and resist the temptations of the enemy.

Understand that sometimes on a fast you can't hear God speak over the sound of your stomach growling. You can't focus on morning devotions for thinking about oatmeal. (It is amazing how, during an extended fast, even the most bland foods sound wonderful. Food you would normally pass over on a breakfast buffet suddenly sounds like fine dining.) You want to read the Word, but you have a headache; you are cold and probably tired from the toxins being filtered out of your body. You might feel like you are just physically falling apart, but stay the course and don't let your flesh or the devil shortchange your reward! If there is one thing the devil cannot stand, it is waiting.

While You Wait

Essentially, fasting is waiting on God. One of the most quoted verses from the Book of Isaiah is found in chapter 40: "But those who wait on the LORD shall renew their strength; they shall mount up with wings like eagles, they shall run and not be weary, they shall walk and not faint" (v. 31). You will renew your strength as you wait on Him. Do you see what else happens? You will mount up with wings like eagles, one of the strongest birds God created. Not wings like sparrows or butterflies, but wings like eagles—that's a much more trustworthy claim than any energy drink can make!

There are two kinds of people in this world who need "wings." There are those who have been devastated by horrible events that have left them feeling like their life is over, their hope is crushed. They are caught in the rubble of broken pieces feeling like they will never be put back together again, and they can no longer rise above the circumstances. But God promises that to those who will wait on Him, He will give wings to rise above. He will give you strength to run your race with endurance!

The other type of person who needs wings is the one who is fighting for his or her dreams. Are you relying on your own zeal to make it happen? The problem with that is, you can only get so far. Ultimately you just can't get it off the ground. You've made some leaps, but you have yet to soar. It may be your ministry, your calling, your business, or your marriage. You are trying. You are fighting for it, but somehow you need more. It's kind of like Nehemiah rebuilding the walls of Jerusalem. There is no way he could have accomplished that great task in fifty-two days without first waiting upon the Lord, humbling himself with fasting and prayer. You must back up and sharpen your ax. You have to walk before you can run...but you have to *wait* before you can soar. When you wait on the Lord, He will give you strong wings to soar beyond your limitations.

So what do you do while you wait on the Lord? You be still. I'm not making that up—God said it Himself:

> Be still, and know that I am God;
> I will be exalted among the nations,
> I will be exalted in the earth!

—PSALM 46:10

When you fast, quiet yourself. Get still by turning off the crazy distractions of this life and press in to God's presence. Open God's Word and devour it. God will speak to you through His Word. The Bible contains the answer to every dilemma you face, and if you will read it as you fast, God will speak to you. The Lord instructed Joshua to keep His Word before him and meditate on it day and night. God's Word should become part of your being, changing your inner man to line up with God's will.

Daniel chapter 10 describes an amazing glimpse into what happens in the heavenlies sometimes while we wait. Daniel had been fasting and praying for three weeks, but the answer he waited for was delayed. The angel Gabriel had a message for Daniel, but he was detained battling the prince (demonic principality) of Persia. As Daniel persisted in fasting and prayer, God sent the angel Michael as reinforcement for Gabriel so he could break free and deliver the message to Daniel. Think about that whenever the enemy tempts you to give up on a fast. That is the time to press in like never before! There may be situations in your life, in your family, in your work or ministry where it seems like Satan is so deeply entrenched he will never be ousted. Don't believe the lie. Fast, pray, and wait upon the Lord! As you wait, you will strengthen your inner man, becoming more and more aware of your authority in Christ Jesus over the devil.

Your spirit wants worship, but the flesh wants temporary satisfaction. Your spirit wants to praise and honor God, but the flesh wants to party and live for self. Now you can see why Paul so urgently warns us to "walk in the Spirit, and you shall not fulfill the lust of the flesh" (Gal. 5:16). You can be victorious in the battle between your flesh and spirit, and fasting, prayer, and feeding your spirit on God's Word help accelerate the process.

Zeal to Zero

Remember, Paul is the same one who had so much zeal that he was jailing and even took part in killing Christians until he met Jesus. Then he submitted all those ways of the flesh unto the Spirit. Can God use your zeal? Of course He can, if it is under submission. Do you remember what Peter did in the Garden of Gethsemane when the troops came to arrest Jesus? He yanked out his sword and cut off the ear of the high priest's servant! That was zeal, but it wasn't God's will. Jesus had to rebuke Peter once again, saying, "Put your sword into the sheath. Shall I not drink the cup which My Father has given Me?" (John 18:11). Jesus could have had twelve legions of angels sent to His aid in a heartbeat. But that was not the will of God. That was not how Scripture would be fulfilled.[3] Jesus had already submitted His flesh to the will of the Father when He prayed earlier, "Father, if it is Your will, take this cup away from Me; nevertheless not My will, but Yours, be done" (Luke 22:42).

The Holy Spirit has made it very clear to me on more than one occasion that I cannot do God's will in my own zeal. Our zeal can become a stumbling block based in our own pride. God needs empty vessels—not ones so full of themselves that He can't pour Himself out through them. In the last chapter I talked about prayer connections and how praying is "plugging into" God's assignment and His resources. Few would argue that Elijah was a man who was truly plugged into God. I remember reading a quote from Leonard Ravenhill several years ago, talking about how people who were not accomplishing much for God wanted to ask, "Where is the God of Elijah?" He wrote:

> To the question, "Where is the Lord God of Elijah?" we answer, "Where He has always been—on the throne!" But where are the Elijahs of God? We know Elijah was "a man of like passions as we are," but alas! we are not men of like prayer as he was. One praying man stands as a majority with God! Today God is bypassing men—not because they are too ignorant, but because they are too self-sufficient. Brethren, our abilities are our handicaps, and our talents our stumbling blocks![4]

We will not accomplish God's will with self-sufficient, arrogant zeal. Remember the young lumberjack I spoke of earlier? Full of zeal! The problem was, it was zeal without knowledge. Proverbs 19:2 warns, "It is not good to have zeal without knowledge, nor to be hasty and miss the way" (NIV). If he had known to take time to sharpen his ax and keep the edge on it, he would have more than likely beaten the older lumberjack. But there is that problem again: the fact that far too often we want to rely on our own strength, our own ability, our own zeal to get something done for God.

When you read about the prophet Elijah, beginning in 1 Kings chapter 17, you see him humbly and consistently following God's assignment. Elijah tells Ahab there will be no rain, and God tells Elijah to go hide himself by the river and he would be brought meals of bread and meat by ravens. (Now that is an odd fast!) Then the river dried up due to the drought that God had Elijah prophesy. I believe Elijah had to wait there on the Lord for his next assignment. In fact, I imagine as that river became increasingly narrow, Elijah began praying more and more loudly! God then sent him to a widow's house where He provided flour and oil for her to make bread for Elijah, her son, and herself so they could survive until the drought was over. Some of us carboholics wouldn't have any problem with a "bread-only" fast. But then God sent his faithful prophet to confront Ahab, who had searched high and low for him in order to have him killed.

> God needs empty vessels—not ones
> so full of themselves that He can't
> pour Himself out through them.

Elijah challenged Ahab and Jezebel's 450 prophets of the false god Baal in a dramatic showdown, and then he had them all slaughtered. Soon after he prayed for rain to once again be released in the land. Elijah was accomplishing mighty things for God! Then Jezebel heard all that had happened and sent word to Elijah that she would have him killed within twenty-four hours. Suddenly Elijah feared for his life. The Bible says, "And when he *saw that*, he arose and ran for his life, and went to Beersheba, which belongs to Judah, and left his servant there" (1 Kings 19:3 emphasis added). Something about the demonic drive behind her words caused him to "see" it, or to envision it happening. He disconnected from the Spirit of God for a moment and let his mind agree with and empower that evil woman's threat. He got his eyes on his own flesh. After he dropped off his servant nearly eighty miles away, he went into the wilderness and told God, "I give up." He was done. He'd had enough. He wanted to die.

It makes me think of Paul's word to the Galatians: "Are you so foolish? Having begun in the Spirit, are you now being made perfect by the flesh?" (Gal. 3:3). When you stop praying, you start operating in the flesh, and it is just a matter of time before weariness and fear begin to overtake your life. This is what happens to prayerless, carnal Christians who live in the flesh, driven by religious zeal instead of the Spirit of God. But there is hope. Like Elijah, you can stop and replenish. You can sharpen your ax and get your edge back! Human zeal puts on a good show, but you cannot accomplish God's will without the anointing of the Spirit. Religion is done in the flesh. Relationship is *only* accomplished in the Spirit. "For as many as are led by the Spirit of God, these are sons of God" (Rom. 8:14).

Elijah hid himself under a tree in the desert and asked to die. It was his lowest moment, right on the heels of delivering one of the most powerful blows to the enemy. When God confronted him, he said, "I have been very zealous for the LORD God of hosts; for the children of Israel have forsaken Your covenant, torn down Your altars, and killed Your prophets with the sword. I alone am left; and they seek to take my life" (1 Kings 19:10). Elijah got his eyes on his own limitations and off of the purpose and power of God. But God hadn't even begun to use him yet! You may need to go sit under a tree for a day or two. But don't ever believe the lie that God is done with you. The Lord sent him an angel to feed and strengthen him. Then He sent Elijah on a forty-day fast through the wilderness. At the end of that fast and journey, Elijah came back in the power and anointing of the Holy Spirit and had a fresh message for old Jezebel. He turned the tables and gave her a real graphic picture to think about when he prophesied that the dogs would eat her outside of the palace.[5]

Now, here is very noteworthy evidence regarding the power of humbling yourself through prayer and fasting. Elijah was sent to pronounce judgment on Ahab and Jezebel for their ongoing wickedness, their blasphemy, murdering the prophets of God, and their evil plot to kill

Naboth in order to possess his land. Elijah made plain to Ahab all the sins he had done against the Lord and the Lord's anointed, how severely the Lord had judged and condemned him, and how he and his entire family would be destroyed. And then a surprising thing happened:

> So it was, when Ahab heard those words, that he tore his clothes and put sackcloth on his body, *and fasted* and lay in sackcloth, and went about mourning. And the word of the LORD came to Elijah the Tishbite, saying, "See how Ahab has humbled himself before Me? Because he has humbled himself before Me, I will not bring the calamity in his days. In the days of his son I will bring the calamity on his house."
>
> —1 KINGS 21:27–29, EMPHASIS ADDED

In God's eyes, no king of Israel had ever been as wicked as Ahab. But because Ahab humbled himself with fasting, God acknowledged it. The Lord eased the verdict on Ahab's sins just slightly so that he wouldn't see the full punishment within his own lifetime.

It is astounding to me how faithful God is even when we are not!

When you let your weakness bring you to your knees and you humble yourself with fasting and prayer, God can replenish you. Elijah got his anointing back after he fasted. He moved once again in the authority to conquer

135

the enemy rather than running from the enemy's threats. Maybe you have fought some battles so long that you just don't think you have any ability left to fight. Don't give up. Pray on; press in. There are bigger weapons in the Spirit that you haven't even begun to learn how to use yet. Prayer and fasting are like opening up the "atomic weapons arsenal" in heaven against the enemy!

You don't have to live in weakness, coddling your flesh. This is war. It's time to pull out the atomic weapons and get serious with God. When you fast and pray, ask the Holy Spirit to fill you again with fresh anointing. When you are battle weary, it is so easy to just give up. But if you will fast, it will replenish your spirit and your authority in Christ. Pray until you feel that authority. Pray until the Spirit touches and fills you afresh. Pray until you get broken before God.

Fast With Purpose

When you draw closer to God, He draws closer to you.[6] In the same way, when you get serious with God, He gets serious with you. I've always admired David's attitude when he hit the battlefield where his brothers and the armies of Israel cowered in fear from enduring forty days of Goliath the Philistine's threats. This young man, full of passion for God, pipes up and asks, "Is there not a cause?" (1 Sam. 17:29). David was full of passion for God's glory. He was intimate with God and knew that the Spirit of the Lord empowered him at times when necessary, like when he had to protect his father's flock from a lion and, on another occasion, a bear. David, who could measure himself by God's measure rather than man's standard, could see that this enemy of God would fall just like the lion and the bear. Saul and the army of Israel could only see themselves in their own eyes, a scary place when facing a threatening, sword-wielding giant enemy.

When you choose to fast, fast with a cause. Deep in your heart, determine the reason you're fasting, and then write down your cause. It is important to keep your focus. That is why I designed the Fasting Contract that we use at Free Chapel, which is available online. One of the first things to fill out on that contract is My Reason for Fasting.

What is on your heart for this fast? Is it for your family? Is it your desire to draw closer to God? Is it the need for financial breakthrough? Is it for a healing? Are you fasting because you are afraid and have so many problems surrounding you that you don't know what else to do? Define your reason, and then write it down. Do not enter a fast casually, with a hit-or-miss attitude. That is a sure recipe for failure. Never enter into a spiritual fast casually, because if you're casual about it, God will be casual about it. Plan to succeed from the start. Pray and ask God what He wants you to do. Prayerfully determine the length and

you use a smooth stone to polish and hone that steel to a razor-fine edge. It is a process that takes time. It is like the middle part of the fast—you're not done. The final step in getting your edge back is to take the oil and gently rub it from the top to the bottom of that sharp blade in order to get all the fragments, shavings, and dirt off of it. You could think about that "DIRT" as an acronym:

D—Disobedience
I—Ignorance (zeal without knowledge)
R—Rebellion
T—The tongue (words of doubt and unbelief)

Then, you are ready to swing that ax under the anointing of the Lord!

Chapter 8

Flourishing in Troubled Times

I t doesn't take long for anyone to lose his or her edge looking at the condition of the US economy these days. Most of us "over-forty-somethings" can remember the Nixon/Ford/Carter presidency days of the seventies. Nixon's decisions kicked off a rough decade, starting with a devalued dollar and lower gold prices, followed by peak unemployment and recession, ending with peak inflation and angry gas lines. I remember those gas lines. Even as a kid I could sense the insecurity that my family felt regarding the economy in those days. Kids today have watched as their mom and dad have lost their jobs—and many have lost their homes to foreclosure—all at record rates. People have seen their savings run out and their investments plunge almost overnight in some cases. My heart has been heavy as I've witnessed the economy in America sink deeper into crisis. But I want to encourage you—now more than ever— to believe God for His provision. I see evidence throughout Scripture that the men and women of God who pressed in with fasting and prayer, even in difficult times, flourished. God provides. He provides because He is faithful to His Word. He promised:

> The righteous shall flourish like a palm tree,
> He shall grow like a cedar in Lebanon.
> Those who are planted in the house of the LORD
> Shall flourish in the courts of our God.
> They shall still bear fruit in old age;
> They shall be fresh and flourishing,
> To declare that the LORD is upright;
> He is my rock, and there is no unrighteousness
> in Him.
>
> —PSALM 92:12–15

I don't know about you, but I take much more comfort and place much more faith in the promises of God than I do in the promises of government—any government!

Most species of palm trees grow in desert climates. They become firmly rooted even in shifting sand, by design. They tolerate high temperatures, little rainfall, and high winds. And I really liked this part: palm trees produce better fruit in their old age. Palms can flourish where other trees would wither and die, and God promises that the righteous, those in right standing with Him, will flourish where others would wither. God designed the root system of palms differently than that of most other trees. Instead of the roots tapering and becoming smaller the farther away they get from the trunk, they stay about the same size. So these big, thick roots make their way far below the hot, dry shifting sands and lock into the nutrient-providing solid foundation below. Not only that, but unlike most trees that have a woody-dead outer layer, the entire trunk of a palm is alive, allowing it to be very flexible, bending with even hurricane-force winds.[1]

I believe fasting is necessary to help us sink our roots ever deeper into the solid foundation of God's promises so that we can withstand the storms as they come and continue to be fruitful. As the apostle Paul wrote, "As you have therefore received Christ Jesus the Lord, so walk in Him, rooted and built up in Him and established in the faith, as you have been taught, abounding in it with thanksgiving" (Col. 2:6–7). Storms will come. Some storms are transitional in nature. Transition is a season that few enjoy because of the storms it unleashes.

Change Can Be Troublesome

The changing economy has certainly stirred up a lot of destructive storms in the past few years, forcing families to transition from a place where things were safe and pleasurable to the unknown and unfamiliar. The disciples were content watching Jesus heal the sick and cast out demons with a word along the shore of the Sea of Galilee. But later that night He told them to hop in the boat and set sail for the other shore. That is when things got a little dicey as a major storm stirred up high waves and wind, tossing around their once comfortable little boat and filling it up until it nearly capsized. But when they looked around during the worst part of that storm, they didn't see Jesus with a bucket scooping water out of the boat. They didn't see Him strapping on a life jacket. Jesus was in the back of the boat sound asleep! When they woke Him up to save them, He pointed out their lack of faith and spoke to the wind and waves, calming the storm.[2]

Sometimes it seems as if life is nothing but one big transition. Just about the time you get good at something you've been doing for a while, a shift takes place, and suddenly you are facing brand-new territory and unchartered waters. Life throws scenarios at you that you could never plan for or dream up. Change is a difficult process. But when transitional storms come, they test and strengthen your root system. Without spending time waiting on God when the skies are cloudless, many are completely unprepared to handle the storms of life. Paul said he had learned how to be content no matter the circumstances.[3] That is a goal we should all set our hearts to attain! He knew how to hit bottom and be content, and to soar on the heights and still be content. Face it; sometimes you're the "big dog," and other times you feel more like the fire hydrant. There are times I can look back on in my life where it seemed like everything worked perfectly and exceeded all my expectations. There are other times when nothing went right, and I had to reach up to touch rock bottom. The key is to learn to worship, to humble yourself with fasting and prayer, and to seek God's face no matter the transition.

That is why some run aground and capsize their faith. As long as they are abounding, they come to church with their hands raised, ready to stomp, shout, and praise. They are on top of the world…until they hit the bottom of the valley. Then you rarely see them around anymore, and if you do see them, they look like an old lemon, withered and without any joy, feeling as though God has forsaken them. On the other hand, I have seen people serve God faithfully when they are at rock bottom, but as soon as transition brings blessings, promotions, and increase their way, they forget all about the Lord.

That is not how you handle transition! Spending time in fasting and prayer—regardless of your circumstances—is what will help you be rooted and grounded in your faith, ready to weather any storm of the economy, your health, your family, or your job. God can cause you to flourish even during transition, and people who flourish in troubled times have been used to change destinies.

Daniel had been fasting and repenting again for the sins of Israel, the sins that brought about their exile to other nations and the near destruction of Jerusalem in the first place. When the angel Gabriel dropped in on Daniel a second time, he talked to him, encouraging Daniel about future events. One part of the vision that Gabriel gave to Daniel was that Jerusalem would be restored again, and building would continue there "even in troublesome times" (Dan. 9:25). I have never claimed to be a Bible scholar, and like most people, I have yet to discover the depths of some of the mysteries of the Book of Daniel. But that verse always encourages me when I think about God's promises. He will cause the righteous to flourish, to build, to expand their territory even in troublesome times! Even when the economy is crashing, when we fast, pray, and seek God's face, we can receive wisdom and plans and resources to endure and overcome.

Fasting That Changed Destinies

Until we leave this world and cross into the presence of God, we will not know the full impact that unknown, humble, praying saints have had on the destiny of cities, nations, and cultures. We need to meditate on the examples that we do have because they are intended to inspire and encourage us to step out of our own routines and pursue God in like manner. Look at what happened in Nineveh. God chose one man named Jonah to go and preach repentance to the people of the vast city that stood as the capital of the Assyrian empire. The wickedness of the city had come up before the Lord, so He sent a reluctant prophet to go and pronounce judgment. Aren't you glad that we serve a merciful God? Jonah finally stopped procrastinating, entered the city, and started proclaiming, "Yet forty days, and Nineveh shall be overthrown!" (Jon. 3:4). Needless to say, his words created quite a stir. Even though that city was so large that it took three days to cross, word spread very quickly.

> So the people of Nineveh believed God, proclaimed a fast, and put on sackcloth, from the greatest to the least of them. Then word came to the king of Nineveh; and he arose from his throne and laid aside his robe, covered himself with sackcloth and sat in ashes. And he caused it to be proclaimed and published throughout Nineveh by the decree of the king and his nobles, saying, Let neither man nor beast, herd nor flock, taste anything; do not let them eat, or drink water. But let man and beast be covered with sackcloth, and cry mightily to God; yes, let every one turn from his evil way and from the violence that is in his hands. Who can tell if God will turn and relent, and turn away from His fierce anger, so that we may not perish?
>
> —JONAH 3:5–9

Nineveh was a Gentile city, and the people there were not known to be God-fearing. But the king took the prophet's warning so seriously that he even ordered the animals to fast! They had seen the judgment of God in other lands enough to know that He wasn't kidding. Conviction hit hard, and the people repented, *humbling themselves* with prayer and fasting. As a result, God relented. The entire city was spared, at least in that generation, because they fasted and cried out to God with repentant hearts. Their final judgment and destruction did not come until roughly two hundred years later, after God once again saw their wickedness and sent prophet after prophet to warn them. But that time the people refused to turn from their wickedness and were destroyed.

> Spending time in fasting and prayer—regardless of your circumstances—is what will help you be rooted and grounded in your faith, ready to weather any storm of the economy, your health, your family, or your job.

We have already covered how a three-day fast spared the Jewish people from total annihilation in Esther's day. When they humbled themselves before the Lord, instead of defeat and shame, there was honor and promotion.

Jehoshaphat looked up one day to find himself surrounded by fierce enemies. But in 2 Chronicles 20, he declared a fast, and the Lord heard the cry of the people and fought *for* them, defeating the enemy.

In 1620, Christians fleeing the religious oppression of England landed along the shores of what is now Plymouth, Massachusetts. History records that it was very difficult that first year for the Pilgrims who formed Plymouth Colony. About half of them died of starvation over the winter. They were at a severe disadvantage because most of them knew nothing of how to farm, hunt, or fish in this new, wild territory.

A Native American who came to be known by the Pilgrims simply as Squanto helped them plant crops. He showed them how to fertilize the crops with fish that they caught. He also tried to help to mend very bad relations between the settlers and the other native tribes. Things were looking more promising until the spring of 1623, when a severe drought threatened all of the crops that would sustain them through the winter. Their lives hung in the balance without rain. They prayed and encouraged each other with specific verses from Scripture, like:

> Fear not, for I am with you;
> Be not dismayed, for I am your God.
> I will strengthen you,

Yes, I will help you,
I will uphold you with My righteous right hand.

—Isaiah 41:10

They clung to such promises in faith that God would indeed hear their cry and help. William Bradford, the governor of Plymouth Colony, noted this portion of Scripture in his journal, reflecting on the events of that time. It hadn't rained for nearly three months, so Bradford called for a fast. The Pilgrims agreed and fasted from sunrise throughout the day. The sky remained clear, without the promise of rain. But by that nightfall, clouds like no one had seen in months began to form. Before long a gentle, soaking rain began to thoroughly replenish the land and their crops. The neighboring Indians, afflicted by the same drought, were amazed at how the Pilgrims' God answered the Pilgrims' dire need when they humbled themselves and prayed. The miracle made a lasting impression on the neighboring Indians. The Pilgrims were spared because of a fast.

Prayer and fasting has birthed many revivals that brought about significant change. The revival that swept the Hebrides in Scotland was often credited to Duncan Campbell's preaching. But he was quick to give credit to two praying elderly ladies who had a burden for the people of their town, especially the young people who ignored anything to do with God. The two women received a vision from God and shared it with some of the young ministers there, encouraging them to join in prayer at least two nights a week. After three weeks, one of those men became convicted in his own heart that God would not use men without "clean hands and a pure heart" (Ps. 24:4) to reach others. As the men in that prayer meeting repented and cried out to God, His Spirit swept the entire town with mighty conviction. A Spirit-born revival shook that area for the next three years, and nearly everyone on the island was born again, young and old, most before they even reached the church building.[4]

Bill Bright, the founder of Campus Crusade for Christ (now known as Cru), was a man who understood the power of fasting and prayer. He wrote about a personal conviction to fast that hit him in the early 1990s:

> In the spring and summer of 1994, I had a growing conviction that God wanted me to fast and pray for forty days for revival in America and for the fulfillment of the Great Commission in obedience to our Lord's command....As I began my fast, I was not sure I could continue for forty days. But my confidence was in the Lord to help me. Each day His presence encouraged me to continue. The longer I fasted, the more I sensed the presence of the Lord. The Holy Spirit refreshed my soul and spirit, and I experienced the joy of the Lord as seldom before. Biblical

truths leaped at me from the pages of God's Word. My faith soared as I humbled myself and cried out to God and rejoiced in His presence. This proved to be the most important forty days of my life. As I waited upon the Lord, the Holy Spirit gave me the assurance that America and much of the world will, before the end of the year 2000, experience a great spiritual awakening.[5]

America did in fact experience a great wave of awakening, revival, and evangelism during the 1990s—and I am convinced there is more, much more, that God has in store as we take up the call to fast and pray for this nation! When the people of God truly take hold of fasting and intercession, we will see things begin to change. Even though the economy feels like a turbulent storm, God promised that the righteous will flourish. We are ambassadors of Christ equipped and called to impact this world with heaven's purposes. When you fast and pray, you will see your own circumstances sustained even in troublesome times. Then you can impact your community, your town, your city, your state…and ultimately the nation.

Standing in the Gap

We refer to "the Daniel fast" quite often for what he did and didn't eat on those twenty-one-day fasts. But we need to also look at how he prayed during those times. God had turned His people over to their enemies because of their unrepentant hearts and continued adultery against Him with other gods. Daniel's life was turned upside down when he was taken captive to Babylon because of the sins of Israel. Yet as Daniel prayed, he was confessing the sins of the entire nation to the Lord as if they were his own personal sins. He prayed, "Then I set my face toward the Lord God to make request by prayer and supplications, with fasting, sackcloth, and ashes.…All this disaster has come upon us; yet we have not made our prayer before the LORD our God, that we might turn from our iniquities and understand Your truth" (Dan. 9:3, 13). Daniel fasted and stood in the gap not just for his own needs but also for the entire nation. That is true intercession. He understood what God required and was willing to humble himself and seek the Lord. It was during that time that he heard from Gabriel about the rebuilding of Jerusalem in troubled times.

Solemn Assembly

The rebuilding of Jerusalem started years later when Nehemiah began fasting and praying for God to make a way for him to go and repair the city's wall and gates. They were not merely broken; they were heaps of burned rubble that had been untouched for decades. When his work began, the enemy was quick to arrive. Have you ever noticed that? It seems like any time you get direction from the Lord for a particular work that He wants accomplished, the enemy stirs up "troublesome times."

Remember: The focus of the enemy is *always* to cause the work of God to cease!

In Nehemiah's case, the attacks started with angry ridicule to cause the people of Jerusalem to doubt their feeble abilities. Sound familiar? Have you set out to do something for the Lord, and circumstances or criticism had you doubting yourself before you could even get started? Fast, pray, and press on with the work God has called you to do.

Of course, when ridicule didn't stop the work, the enemy threatened to fight against the people of Jerusalem. But Nehemiah remained more impressed with God's promises than he was by the enemy's threats. He had spent time getting the heart of God on the task and knew what he was there to do. Instead of becoming discouraged, he armed some of the men for battle as they built the wall and kept going.

> Remember: The focus of the enemy is *always* to cause the work of God to cease!

When the threats didn't slow down the rebuilding, the enemy plotted to sneak inside the city, saying, "They will neither know nor see anything, till we come into their midst and kill them and cause the work to cease" (Neh. 4:11). Nehemiah rallied the people not to fall for that threat either, and the rebuilding continued.

Encouraged by the success of the wall being restored, Israelites who had been scattered far and wide for years began to make their way back to Jerusalem. Many who had been born in captivity needed to learn the ways of God, so they gathered daily to hear Ezra read from the Bible. They joyously celebrated their first feast together after the walls were rebuilt, the Feast of Tabernacles. At the end of the weeklong celebration, they called a solemn assembly on the eighth day to fast and pray.

> The children of Israel were assembled with fasting, in sackcloth, and with dust on their heads. Then those of Israelite lineage separated themselves from all foreigners; and they stood and confessed their sins and the iniquities of their fathers. And they stood up in their place and read from the Book of the Law of the LORD their God for one-fourth of the day; and for another fourth they confessed and worshiped the LORD their God.
>
> —NEHEMIAH 9:1–3

The Feast and the fast that followed were ordained by God and had a lasting impact on the reformation of Jerusalem. There are several elements in this fast that we can glean from to "supercharge" our own season of fasting and consecration.

Assemble

The first element of this fast was that all the people stopped what they were doing and came together in common unity, with a common purpose. When you gather with other believers, even if it is just a couple of friends whom you ask to fast with you about an issue, it is powerful. It also gives you a "buddy system," so when you get weak and start seeing visions of french fries, you have a friend to call who will pray you off the edge. Plug in with other believers when you are fasting and praying for a situation.

Separate

The Israelites separated themselves from others in the land, those who did not follow the Lord. They needed to come away from outside influences that would have hindered their consecration to the Lord. In the same way, it is important to separate yourself from the things of this world. Turn off the entertainment. Walk away from the computer and e-mails once in a while. Fasting is not just about food; it's also about those things that hinder your consecration and focus on Him. What good is "not eating" if you are still spending hours with your eyes glued to the TV and ears filled with ungodly music? Your spirit becomes especially open during a fast. You are open to whatever you are feeding your spirit...the things of God as well as ungodly things.

Confess

Notice that "they stood and confessed their sins and the iniquities of their fathers" (Neh. 9:2). When you begin to fast, begin to repent. God will bring sins and iniquities to your attention as you fast and pray, times you've compromised, words you've spoken, your attitudes and actions that aren't rooted in His love, people you have wronged. As you fast, be quick to repent of things that come to mind. As John wrote, "If we confess our sins, He is faithful and just to forgive us our sins and to cleanse us from all unrighteousness" (1 John 1:9).

The Word

When you fast, you empty yourself. When you repent, you empty yourself. You need to fill those voids with the Word of God. Notice that they "stood up in their place and read from the Book of the Law of the Lord their God for one-fourth of the day" (Neh. 9:3). As they fasted, they gathered to hear the Word of God read. Faith comes by hearing the Word! When you fast, read your Bible. Consume it.

Worship

Finally it says, "For another fourth they confessed and worshiped the Lord their God" (Neh. 9:3). They had assembled together, they separated from ungodly influences, they confessed their sins, and for half the day they read God's Word, confessed, and worshiped. For clarity, "confessed" in this instance refers to confessing the greatness of God. The people were speaking forth the truths and promises of God's Word as they worshiped. While you're fasting, always confess the truths and promises of God over yourself and your family. Worship is critical during a fast.

"Afterward"

The Book of Joel begins with a description of a land so desolate even the palm tree has withered. He describes a severe judgment that results in famine and utter devastation. Yet God offers a glimmer of hope even to a people deemed worthy of such destruction when He says, "Turn to Me with all your heart, with fasting, with weeping, and with mourning" (Joel 2:12). Joel calls the people to, "Rend your heart, and not your garments; return to the LORD your God, for He is gracious and merciful, slow to anger, and of great kindness; and He relents from doing harm" (v. 13). The book begins with destruction and ends with promise *after* the people have called a sacred assembly with serious fasting and prayer. Joel 2:28 says, "And it shall come to pass afterward that I will pour out My Spirit on all flesh; your sons and your daughters shall prophesy, your old men shall dream dreams, your young men shall see visions."

The stormy economy of late has caused people to lose jobs, houses—some have lost everything. Are you living in what seems like devastation? It is time to fast, repent, and seek the Lord. I believe in "afterward"! I believe God will give you fresh dreams and vision for your life. Even though you are walking through troublesome times today, relief is coming.

As the church, the people of God, it is time to shake off the restraints of "political correctness" when it comes to passion for the Lord. God is not moved by political correctness; He is moved by our passion for Him. From Genesis to Revelation, taking up your cross, following the Lord, turning from wickedness, and dying to the flesh are all part of being a Christian. But the church is becoming so carnal that it is not uncommon to hear those who fast, pray, and seek His face referred to as "fanatics." It's not nutty to go without food for a set portion of time so that we can know God better. What's nutty is settling instead for a mediocre, lukewarm relationship with Jesus.

As a nation, we need to take seriously the warnings of God. He will send relief when His people do their part to humble themselves with fasting and prayer, seeking His face. "For since the beginning of the world men have not heard nor perceived by the ear, nor has the eye seen any God besides You, who acts for the one who waits for Him" (Isa. 64:4). The people of God are beginning to take seriously the call to fast and pray. This past year 300,000 Christians around the world joined Free Chapel in our first of the year twenty-one-day fast to honor the Lord! Most start with three days of a strict fast, taking only water and juice, and then convert to the "Daniel fast" for the remaining twenty-one days, abstaining from all meats, sweets, and breads. But what you do or do not eat on a spiritual fast is only part of the equation. The other part of a fast is repenting and seeking His face. We need to assemble, to consecrate ourselves from worldly distractions, confess our sins and the sins of our nation, dig deeply into God's Word, and worship Him with passion and praise!

> As the church, the people of God, it is time to shake off the restraints of "political correctness" when it comes to passion for the Lord.

Chapter 9

The Main Dish

There are a couple of restaurants in Missouri, and one in Alabama, that have developed a most unusual means of serving their customers. In fact, their method has become their trademark over the years. Established in 1949, Lambert's Café was known for good down-home cooking. But in 1976, it became Lambert's Café: "The Only Home of the Throwed Rolls." It seems that the proprietor, Norman Ray Lambert, was too busy one day to get more rolls to a customer's table. Impatient to get his delicious, fresh-from-the-oven yeast roll, the customer yelled, "Oh just throw the darn thing." So Norman obliged with a good toss, the customer caught the hot roll, and a trademark was born. When you visit one of their three locations, waiters come out all day long with trays of hot rolls, fresh from the oven, and begin slinging the five-inch-wide rolls through the air to waiting customers. It gets everyone's attention as hands go up all over the restaurant beckoning the waiter to fire away. Most of the time the rolls are caught by hand, but occasionally one slips through your fingers and slams into the head of the person at the next table.

According to their website, the bread ovens at Lambert's blaze nonstop for the full twelve-hour shift, turning out an average of 500 rolls every day, over 2.2 million rolls a year. With that much excitement and attention given to flying hunks of bread, you might think it's the main course. But of course, it is not. The "throwed rolls" are only a side dish, an add-on for those who come to enjoy a huge plate of ribs, catfish, fried chicken, country-fried steak, or other main dishes.

Bread has taken a backseat since ancient times. Then it was regarded not only as a main source of nutrition but also as having a symbolic meaning. Our wheat crops today originated in the Fertile Crescent area in the Middle East, known as the cradle of civilization and the place Abraham called home. As part of the curse for man's sin, God told Adam, "In the sweat of your face you shall eat bread till you return to the ground" (Gen. 3:19). He was referring to mankind having to labor to work the land and cultivate crops of wheat that would provide their primary source of nutrition. Long before our TV commercials proclaimed, "Beef: it's what's for dinner," the slogan would have instead been more like, "Bread: it's what's for dinner."

Unlike those delicious, fluffy yeast rolls from Lambert's Café however, the bread of the Bible was often made without yeast or leaven and probably wasn't as fun to toss, unless maybe you threw it like a Frisbee. God used yeast symbolically to illustrate the power of sin in the life of His people, that even a little would puff up the whole lump of dough. Years later Paul warned the Corinthians about their pride, saying:

> Do you not know that a little leaven leavens the whole lump? Therefore purge out the old leaven, that you may be a new lump, since you truly are unleavened. For indeed Christ, our Passover, was sacrificed for us. Therefore let us keep the feast, not with old leaven, nor with the leaven of malice and wickedness, but with the unleavened bread of sincerity and truth.
>
> —1 CORINTHIANS 5:6–8

When the Lord and two angels appeared to Abraham, he rushed over to them and said, "My Lord, if I have now found favor in Your sight, do not pass on by Your servant. Please let a little water be brought, and wash your feet, and rest yourselves under the tree. And I will bring *a morsel of bread*, that you may refresh your hearts" (Gen. 18:3–5 emphasis added). They agreed, and Sarah made bread for them quickly. It is interesting to me that, even though Abraham also served them the meat of a young calf, it was the bread that was intended to refresh the men. When they left, the two angels visited Abraham's nephew, Lot, to warn him of the pending destruction of Sodom. Lot made cakes of unleavened bread for them also.[1]

Years later, when God delivered the Israelites from slavery in Egypt, they were given specific instructions on what to eat that final night, the night their homes would be "passed over" as an angel of death destroyed all the firstborn in Egypt. They were to "be ready," with no time for dough to rise, so part of the Passover meal was, and continues to be, unleavened bread. Then they set about wandering in the desert for forty years, which makes it hard to plant and harvest wheat for bread. So the Lord said to Moses, "Behold, I will rain bread from heaven for you. And the people shall go out and gather a certain quota every day, that I may test them, whether they will walk in My law or not" (Exod. 16:4). They ate that "bread of heaven" daily for the duration of their time in the desert.

Bread was a big deal! It wasn't some "take it or leave it" side option like today. Can you imagine a husband coming home to his wife and hearing her say, "Honey, I've worked all day long preparing a marvelous meal for your dinner." You are starving, so you can't wait to dig into this "feast" your wife has prepared. You sit down at the table to find bread. That's all. Just bread. That might have been exciting three thousand years ago, but not so much now. Today you can go to a restaurant such as Carrabba's, and one of the first things they bring to your table is a basket of warm bread to dip into olive oil and spices. The bread is complimentary. It's just an appetizer provided to tide you over until the better food arrives. You can eat some or not, because it is not the main meal. But in ancient times you didn't pass on the bread without going hungry.

The Old Testament is full of references to bread and its significance in the culture. God told the Israelites, "If you walk in My statutes and keep My commandments, and perform them…you shall eat your bread to the full, and dwell in your land safely" (Lev. 26:3–5). He shall supply all your needs! Even in these verses in Leviticus, keeping God's commandments and walking in obedience related to having all that you needed.

Even sharing your bread with others had meaning. It is part of God's chosen fast to share your bread with the hungry.[2] In that culture, breaking bread literally meant to take the fresh loaf in your hands and tear or break it rather than use a knife to divide the loaf. Sharing what you had by your own hand gave sharing a common meal a more personal, intimate atmosphere. Jesus frequently "broke bread" with His disciples and others. He fed crowds of people after giving thanks and breaking bread, and then multiplying it so that there was enough for everyone who was hungry. Larger loaves of bread were broken by hand and passed about, and people would tear their share into smaller pieces used to dip into a common bowl of meat and vegetables or other dish. In fact, at what we now refer to as the "Last Supper," John asked Jesus who it was that would betray Him. Jesus said, "'It is he to whom I shall give a piece of bread when I have dipped it.' And having dipped the bread, He gave it to Judas Iscariot, the son of Simon" (John 13:26).

I AM the Bread of Life

Now, think about how important bread was in the history of the Israelites as we look at John chapter 6. Jesus's words in this chapter were pivotal even for some of His followers because they could not accept it when He claimed to be "the Bread of Life." The chapter begins with Jesus multiplying five small loaves of barley bread and two small fish that a little boy in the crowd was saving for his lunch. Jesus broke the bread, gave thanks, and fed the entire crowd of more than five thousand who had gathered to hear Him teach. Afterward, the people followed Jesus to the next place, not because they saw a miracle, but because they got a free lunch. Then they asked what sign He would do! He more than rattled a few cages when He replied:

> "Most assuredly, I say to you, Moses did not give you the bread from heaven, but My Father gives you the true bread from heaven. For the bread of God is He who comes down from heaven and

gives life to the world." Then they said to Him, "Lord, give us this bread always." And Jesus said to them, "I am the bread of life. He who comes to Me shall never hunger, and he who believes in Me shall never thirst."

—John 6:32–35

What a statement! Remember, bread was not merely an afterthought or a side dish to the people who heard His words. Bread was the *main part* of their diet. When Jesus said, "I am the bread of life," in that culture, it got their attention. He was trying to get them to understand, "You need Me every day. You need Me not just on Sunday. You need Me every hour. You need Me every minute. You can't make it without Me. I'm the bread of life. I'm the central issue of your life. Without Me, without bread, you'll perish." I can do without a lot of things, but I cannot do anything without Jesus. He's not a side salad. He's not something at the end of the table in a basket that I can take or leave. He is the source of life.

Drive-Through Drama (or Trauma!)

I believe that most of the men reading this will understand what I'm about to share. That's because, deep down, men don't enjoy drive-through ordering. At least not men with a carload of people. I've had experiences, especially when the kids were younger, that left me never wanting to go to a drive-through ever again. My kids are nearly all grown, but the process still rattles my nerves. Once, when Cherise was out of town, I dared swing by a drive-through on the way home from church with all the kids. They were all very little at the time. To avoid having a carload of people screaming and changing orders at the last minute, I stopped to have all of them tell me what they wanted before we ever got to the microphone to order. On this particular stop, the process wasn't going well. I finally got frustrated and told the girl on the other end of the speaker that I wanted five kiddie burger meals with nothing on the bun but ketchup. I pulled forward, paid for my order, took the bags from her, and quietly drove home. My oldest, Courteney, was helping get everyone's burgers distributed when she said in a bewildered tone, "Daddy, there's no meat on these buns." Sure enough, the girl at the drive-through took me completely literally. They had given me five neatly wrapped buns with nothing but ketchup between them!

> Remember, bread was not merely
> an afterthought or a side dish to the
> people who heard His words.

Perhaps you can understand a little better why I get uptight about ordering at drive-through windows. It gets confusing! Total chaos can erupt in the car. I'll pull up, turn off the radio in the car, have everyone's order all lined up in my mind, command total silence, and place my order with confidence, saying at the very end, "And that will be all, thank you." Then do you know what happens? If you're a dad, you do. The voice comes back over the speaker with, "Would you like a hot apple pie with that?" Now, that can mess everything up really quickly as kids start rethinking orders and add-ons.

But I want you to catch what that statement conveys beyond the up-sell pitch. What she really meant was, "Look, apple pies are not our main dish. Apple pies are not the reason that we're in existence. You've already ordered the main dish that we're known for, but I want to know if you want this one little afterthought of a side dish to go with it."

Drive-Through Christianity

The problem is, the body of Christ has developed a drive-through brand of Christianity of late, where we simply "take it or leave it" at will. Nowhere in the Bible does it say that the Bread of Life is merely a *side dish*!

I think when God looks at our busy lives and sees us going here, going there, working, playing, driving kids to ball games, and enjoying all His blessings, at some point His Spirit cries out, "Do you want some God with that?" We focus on getting an education, getting a degree, following a career path, "Would you like some God with that?" How often do we act as though we can pinch off a little nibble of God here and there, fold the napkin back over the dish, and do our own thing the rest of the week? Have our lives become so full that we only have room for a taste of God on Sunday and maybe Wednesday? Do we come into church so full of the world that we have no room for the Bread of Life, so we hustle out to what we consider to be the main course in our lives? Does He look at our pretty buildings and elaborate programs and say, "Do you want some God with that?" Does He listen to our preaching, to our choir singing, to our clapping hands and ask, "Do you want some God with all this religious routine?"

We need to cultivate a genuine hunger and thirst for the Lord! We cannot focus on fasting and prayer and expect to get far when we have the wrong understanding of Jesus in the first place. Jesus continued to explain to the arguing crowd:

> I am the bread of life. Your fathers ate the manna in the wilderness, and are dead. This is the bread which comes down from heaven, that one may eat of it and not die. I am the living bread which came down from heaven. If anyone eats of this

bread, he will live forever; and the bread that I shall give is My flesh, which I shall give for the life of the world.

—John 6:48–51

When you hunger and thirst after Jesus, you will be filled. Ultimately, life just does not work unless you believe that He is the Son of God, the Bread of Life, the main thing that you need to survive. House or no house, I must have bread. Job or no job, I must have bread. We can take all the other stuff on the table and send it back with the waiter, and just put the "bread" right in the center. That is the important thing—everything else is extra. The Bread of Life is the most important thing in your home, in your family, in your marriage, in your life. I believe we are to diligently pursue the dreams God gives us, but we must never allow that pursuit to eclipse Jesus at the center. "For what profit is it to a man if he gains the whole world, and loses his own soul?" (Matt. 16:26).

Hungry for More in Church

Fasting makes you hungry for what really matters in life. You realize that nothing else will satisfy. I want the Bread of Life more than anything else because everything else leaves me hungry. If that is not true in your life, then it is time to fast and pray until that hunger arises. One of the biggest problems in the church today is that we are so full on everything that the world has to offer that we have nothing to offer a starving world.

As a pastor, I want bread in every service. I don't preach well unless my mouth is full of bread. Our choir and praise team do not sing well unless their mouths are full of bread. There isn't a musician alive who can play well enough to set captives free unless breadcrumbs are falling off his fingers as he plays. They should only be up there full of the Bread of Life. We have many talented people in the church. But greater than talent is the bread. Even if someone can't sing that well or preach that well, if they have been with Jesus, then they have what it takes to touch hearts and change lives! We must get the confusion out of the body of Christ: it's not about having church, or singing, or buildings, or budgets. It's not about religious "stuff." It's all about Jesus. When we get that part right, everything else will follow.

When the Bread of Life is present and that fresh aroma begins to fill the room, people do not want to leave. Paul and Silas were thrown into the inner part of a Roman prison with their feet shackled in chains. But instead of murmuring and complaining filling their mouths, their mouths were full of bread! They were singing and worshiping the Lord even at midnight, and the other inmates were listening. Then an earthquake shook the place and broke the chains of all who were bound, knocking the doors open as well.

The jailer, awakened by all the noise, thought all the prisoners had escaped and was about to kill himself when Paul assured him that they were all there.[3] All of them. Not one prisoner left. Every crook, murderer, and thief remained. I believe the presence of God was so real in that place, that not only did the jailer and his family get saved, but also prisoners who could get up and run chose to stay. That makes me think about Sunday mornings when people are meeting with God at the altars, getting free from addictions, coming to Jesus—while everyone else makes a mass exodus out of the back doors. I love to see times where, even though people can leave, they don't because they recognize the Bread of Life is in the room.

Hungry for More at Home

The Bread of Life needs to be more than a side dish in your home too. Dads, you'll never be the husband and father God designed you to be if He is not the main course in your life. Moms, the same applies for you. If you act like the things of God are just some distasteful obligation, your kids will have no appetite for the things of God. You cannot expect your children to fall in love with something that you constantly criticize.

True confession time—I hate liver and onions. As far as I know, not one of my children has ever tried liver.

Why? Because they have heard Cherise and I both say many times that liver is disgusting and tastes like fried dirt. The only thing I've ever tried that tasted worse was the turtle-claw soup the beautiful people of Peru made for me on my first trip to visit the villages we work with along the Amazon. But that is a different story. My point is, if your kids only hear you talk about what you don't like about church, the preacher, the people, the music…eventually you will have children with no hunger for the Bread of Life.

I love my kids, and I am very proud of each one of them. They have grown up in a home with parents who hate liver—but love fasting. Cherise and I have modeled for them the practice of fasting and prayer whenever we desired to be closer to God, or when there was an emergency that just seemed to call for more than prayer.

One of my daughters was going through a rough time of physical sickness recently. We had prayed over her, and yet she still was struggling to feel better. This went on for several weeks. One Sunday after church she began to feel sick again. She began to pray and felt prompted to call her little brother, Drake, to ask him to pray for her as well. At the time, the rest of us were gathered at Drake's favorite Mexican restaurant waiting to place our order. When his phone rang, he calmly walked away from the table to take his sister's call. When she told him what was wrong, Drake immediately began to pray for her over the phone. Now, at twelve, Drake is usually pretty quiet, all boy, and even a little shy. But he completely understood the situation and prayed with power, claiming her complete healing.

Drake finished the call with his sister and quietly walked back to the table. The waiter was there to take our order, so my wife asked Drake what he wanted for lunch. With no prompting and no discussion he answered, "Nothing. Today I am going to fast over what I just prayed for." My heart melted. There sat my youngest, my son, twelve years old in his favorite restaurant, just as hungry as the rest of us—and his *natural* instinct was to fast because that is what he's grown up with. I don't care if my kids ever eat liver as long as they know how to go after God on their own! All Drake wanted for lunch that day was the Bread of Life. We got a call from our daughter later that evening saying that her condition had changed and she was feeling 100 percent better.

Breadwinners

God gave the Israelites manna in the wilderness to provide for them but also to test them to see if they would follow His statutes. Manna did not fall inside their tents. They had to go out and collect the fresh bread of heaven daily. It would not keep overnight in their tents either. It would rot. To apply that today, it means that you have to be responsible for bringing home the Bread of Life. Preachers can't do it all for you on Sunday morning. You have to go to God daily: "Give us this day our daily bread..."[4] Turn off the television, video games, computers, and cell phones. Declare a fast regarding those things if you have to in order to clear the table of everything but the Bread of Life until you are filled.

Most of us have heard the term *breadwinner* before, used in reference to the one who earned a living in the home. But I want to take it to a different level—who is the one who has the Bread of Life in your home? Moms, dads, are you breadwinners? Meaning, when your children feel sick, do they run to you and say, "Daddy...Mommy, pray for me. I know if you'll just pray, God will touch me." When they encounter difficult problems, do they come to you because you are the one with the Bread of Life at home? Are you standing in the place of the breadwinner in the eyes of your family so that they honor or respect you? Do they see your walk with God daily, so that they will ask you about the Bible and expect you to give them spiritual answers? Do they see their parents fussing and arguing daily, or do they see you building each other up from the Word of God? David meant it literally when he wrote, "I have not seen the righteous forsaken, nor his descendants begging bread" (Ps. 37:25). But I believe there is a spiritual side to that too. Your home should be so filled with the Bread of Life that your children don't need to go elsewhere to get filled up.

Lambert's Café serves great food in a fun atmosphere, but they got on the map because they decided to serve it up a little differently one day. God is calling us out of the routine! Break the mold. Take a few days to fast and pray. Ask the Lord to fill you again. If Jesus Himself taught us to pray, "Give us this day our daily bread," then He promises there is something more of God that we can have today that we did not have yesterday. There will be something fresh tomorrow that today's bread just won't stretch to accommodate. Set your mind on the main dish and go after Him!

Chapter 10

Living Inside Out

One day, being a typical man with ADD tendencies, I got up in a hurry, threw on my clothes quickly, and went to grocery store. I had been walking around the store for a little while when I suddenly realized that I was wearing my shirt inside out. I felt so embarrassed! I quickly left the store and drove home to change. There is just something that makes you feel exposed when you wear your clothes inside out. What a mess!

David, chosen by God, king of the people of God, a worshiper at heart—on the outside—but on the inside he was drowning in sin and his attempts to cover up that sin. For a brief period in his life David understood what it meant to be a hypocrite. The young man who killed a giant and became a king under the favor of God knew what it was like to live a lie. It started simply enough. It started the day his troops were away at war and David stayed home where his eyes and thoughts wandered until they stumbled upon the woman bathing next door. She was the wife of a soldier who was away fighting for his king. The story gets more entangled, however. David conceived a child with the other man's wife. Then he tried to cover it up by sending the soldier home to be with his wife so he would think the child was his own once the news broke. But the soldier was so loyal to his king that his mind was only on defending his country, not on being with his wife. Since that didn't work, David sent the soldier to the front lines of battle to be killed. David then married the widow who was pregnant with his child.

As God told the prophet Samuel before he ever anointed David as king, "Man looks at the outward appearance, but the LORD looks at the heart" (1 Sam. 16:7). In His mercy, the Lord sent a man to confront David, and when David was confronted, he broke. He repented and poured out his heart to the Lord asking for mercy, grace, and forgiveness. We see the depth of his sorrow and repentance about this season in many of his psalms, but especially in Psalm 51. Notice what he states in these verses,

> Behold, You desire truth in the inward parts,
> And in the hidden part You will make me to
> know wisdom....
> Create in me a clean heart, O God,
> And renew a steadfast spirit within me.

> Do not cast me away from Your presence,
> And do not take Your Holy Spirit from me.
>
> —Psalm 51:6, 10–11

If you allow sin to take root in your heart, when the Holy Spirit brings conviction about that sin the only cure is to be cleansed and changed from the inside out. Like David, we must realize that it is not something we can do in our own strength. The cycle has to be broken with brokenness. The only thing David could do was to be broken in repentance before God and ask Him to cleanse him from the inside out.

What's Inside

When it comes to the heart of man, what goes in also comes out. That is why Jesus exposed the Pharisees for their pious religious front. He called them pretenders and hypocrites, saying, "You are like tombs that have been whitewashed, which look beautiful on the outside but inside are full of dead men's bones and everything impure. Just so, you also outwardly seem to people to be just and upright but inside you are full of pretense and lawlessness and iniquity" (Matt. 23:27–28, AMP). They looked the part. They played the role. They religiously went through the motions. But they spent much more attention creating the outward standard than they spent following the inward standard. What is on the inside will show on the outside. Think about it this way: when someone gets sick with the flu and nausea takes hold, that person doesn't need training on how to make what is inside come out. The body knows how to do that all by itself! When you have junk inside—junk comes out. But in like manner, when you have Jesus inside—Jesus comes out.

> If you allow sin to take root in your heart, when the Holy Spirit brings conviction about that sin the only cure is to be cleansed and changed from the inside out.

Later, David boldly proclaims, "Bless the LORD, O my soul; and *all that is within me*, bless His holy name!" (Ps. 103:1, emphasis added). I believe David reached a point where he could bless the Lord with everything that was in him because he was not hiding anything from the eyes of God. His spirit was right. His heart was right. His conscience was clear.

The question is, can everything that is *in you* bless His holy name? Is your heart clean before the Lord today? Can you worship Him in spirit and in truth, or do you have "stuff" on the inside that does not bring glory to Him? If we are to worship God in spirit and in truth as Jesus said, that can only come from deep within a clean heart. It does not come from dead men's bones. Jesus said, "If anyone thirsts, let him come to Me and drink. He who believes in Me, as the Scripture has said, out of his heart will flow rivers of living water" (John 7:37–38). Are there rivers of living water coming out of you, or polluted streams? What are you filling yourself up on? What's on the inside?

I think the longer we serve the Lord, the easier it can be to get caught up in the routine of religion. I have to fight that at times. I feel the pressure to be what I am expected to be outwardly even though I may feel totally drained inside. That is why we have to be careful not to put so much energy into keeping up the outward appearance that before long it's just that—an exterior whitewashing to cover a withering interior. It is dangerous for a person or a ministry to be growing outwardly but shrinking in passion for Jesus inwardly.

If I sense my passion for Jesus beginning to fade, I fast. I can't stress enough how fasting helps you regain the edge when you are growing dull. It immediately helps you get refocused on only those things that really matter and cleanse yourself of the rest. Fasting helps you maintain the inward brokenness that allows God to make your outside match your inside. It's living "inside out." You don't have to fake it on the outside when you are full of the Lord on the inside.

A Shiny Dirtball

There is a Japanese craft know as *hikaru dorodango*, which is the art of taking dirt and gently forming it into a smooth, dense ball by hand and then polishing the surface to a shiny finish. The end product is very beautiful and decorative. But inside—it's still *dirt*. Man was created from the outside in. God reached down, took a handful of dirt, rolled it around in His hands for a bit, and carefully sculpted the form of a man. He created his skin, his bones, his muscles, and his internal organs. We all started out as dirt. But we are not supposed to stay that way. After God finished with the dirt, He worked on the inside by breathing His own breath into the man He created, giving him a living soul. That is why you don't get born again on the outside but on the inside. God is not concerned about how shiny your dirt is! He is concerned with the newness of life on the inside, because that will transform the outside.

Is Your Tag Showing?

Have you ever been standing in line at the grocery store when you notice that the guy in front of you is wearing his T-shirt inside out? If so, it was probably me. You can see the tag. You can see the seams exposed. You wonder if he knows it's that way. You wonder if he did it on purpose. You wonder if you should tell him.

Well, when you begin to live inside out spiritually, others can pick up on some of the same indicators about your life. The first thing exposed is your tag. Let's say your *tag* represents your *t*alents *a*nd *g*ifts. When your life is submitted to God, He makes a place for your talents and gifts to be used for His glory. Living inside out exposes your tag, and you begin walking in the destiny God has for you to fulfill. You may not be a ten-talent person. You may not be a five-talent person. But God gave everyone at least one talent, one gifting, and when you live the life God intended for you, He begins to bring those things to the surface. That is where you discover true meaning and purpose for your life. You can't get that from a high salary. You can only get that from God. When you seek the Lord through fasting and prayer, you empty yourself so He can bring out those things that He put in you for His purposes. When your tag shows, the name of the maker shows as well. Your shirt may be made by Old Navy, Tommy Hilfiger, or Armani, but *you* were made by God!

What about size and content? That's on the tag too. Are you a small, medium, or large believer? Personally, I want to be an extra-large! I want people to be able to see that what I have is real. Are you 100 percent pure or a 75 percent blend of different artificial fibers? I am pretty sure that I have met a few polyester Christians, maybe one or two Styrofoam Christians. I also know some who are more like 25 percent—they are Christians on Sunday in church, but they only praise God in church. They have the act outwardly, but the rest of the week they live the way they want. When you are 100 percent pure, you're living inside out. That is when David could say:

> Search me, O God, and know my heart;
> Try me, and know my anxieties;
> And see if there is any wicked way in me,
> And lead me in the way everlasting.
>
> —Psalm 139:23–24

After God restored him, David *wanted* to expose what was on the inside. He understood that was the only way to truly walk with God. Man may be impressed with the outward demonstration, but God sees the heart. He should be able to shine His spotlight on your soul at any time and see that tag glowing back that reads "100 percent." And He will when you are living inside out.

Seam Stress

Going back to the guy in the grocery store again, when a shirt is inside out, you can see the seams. The seams are the most vulnerable part of a shirt. If you put enough pressure on the seams, you can see the thread that runs through it, holding one piece of fabric to the other. I have seen a lot of people come apart at the "seems" when the pressure was on:

- It seems like God is not real.
- It seems like God is not hearing your prayers.
- It seems like you are the only one living for Jesus.

But when you live inside out, people can watch you go through intense pressure without falling apart. Even though you feel weak and vulnerable just like everybody else, when the temptation to come unraveled and fall to pieces is there, that strong thread of faith holds you together.

No Guts, No Glory?

Let's leave the guy and his shirt at the grocery store and go back to the Old Testament days of the tabernacle for a few minutes. God gave Moses specific instructions on the set up and layout of the tabernacle. Everything had meaning and purpose in its placement and order. There were the outer court, the holy place, and the holy of holies where the presence of God dwelt. When you came in through the only gate into the outer court, one of the first things you would see was the brazen altar, used to burn the sacrifice. For a burnt offering you were to bring a young male without blemish from your herd. The priest would slaughter the animal, cut it up, and put it all on the fire, even the guts.

> After God restored him, David *wanted* to expose what was on the inside. He understood that was the only way to truly walk with God.

How many of us are willing to let God go deep? To let Him just rip us open spiritually and explore the depths, cleaning out everything that doesn't bring Him glory? We don't mind coming to church and looking religious because that keeps God or anyone else from going beyond the surface—the gory, inward parts where our bad attitudes, bitterness, unforgiveness, anger, addictions, and secret sins dwell. We want God to release His glory, but we don't want to release our "gory." It will not work that way. It is time to hit the altar. It is time to say, "Rip me open, Lord, and consume anything that is not of You in the fire of Your holiness."

Coaches press athletes to dig deeper, yelling, "C'mon, boys; no guts, no glory!" They have to dig deep to overcome their opponents not only during the game but also in practice before the game. As a Christian the same rule applies. When you are not willing to get down into the "guts" of the matter, God is not willing to pour out His glory. He doesn't look on the exterior but on what is inside your heart.

I am tired of services where we just go through the motions and leave just as we came. We walk in neatly dressed and groomed, but we have all kinds of junk beneath the surface. We look like those shiny balls of dirt! I believe that if we ever get clean on the inside and start living inside out, then God can release His glory upon His people. Are you ready for a purging? Are you ready for the cleansing of the fire of God? Do you want a fresh filling of His Spirit? Seek Him with fasting and prayer, and ask Him to search your innermost parts as David did.

Just *Don't* Do It

While I am thinking about sports analogies, I may as well play off of the Nike slogan of "Just do it." In this case, however, it has to be "Just *don't* do it." When you make fasting a regular part of your life, your sensitivity to the Holy Spirit increases. Things you have struggled with—gossip, nasty language, filthy music and entertainment, secret sins—you find the mercy and grace to rip those things out of your life. You get to the place where you just don't do it anymore because the presence of God is so much more in your life. It is time to get your edge back and cut these things at the root. Clean out the "hidden things" that are not hidden to God.

If you are a single person out on a date, keep your mind and hands where they belong. You can't sinfully gratify the flesh and ask God to release His glory in your life. If you are a young girl or young guy who is living for God, and you're getting pressure from your peers to lose your virginity like everyone else, just don't do it. Tell your so-called friends, "I can be like you any day. But you can try for the rest of your life, and you'll never be able to get back what I still have." Virginity is a package you can open only once. The sin of fornication, sex outside of marriage, is a sin different from every other sin. Your body is sacred. As Paul wrote, "Do you not know that your body is the temple (the very sanctuary) of the Holy Spirit Who lives within you, Whom you have received [as a Gift] from God? You are not your own, you were bought with a price [purchased with a preciousness and paid for, made His own]. So then, honor God and bring glory to Him in your body" (1 Cor. 6:19–20, AMP).

Your body is God's private property. If you look me in the eye and tell me that you love and respect me, but then you go outside and key my car, ruining the paint—you aren't respecting my property! That sends the message that you aren't truly respecting me either. The same goes with your body or the body of someone else. I want to be a pleasing aroma to God. In the Old Testament, the smell of those old gory guts being burned up on the brazen altar was a pleasing fragrance to God. The sin was being atoned for, and He would be able to pour out His glory in the camp.

I was preaching about these things at Free Chapel once and decided to use a visual aid to really bring the point home. I had one of my helpers get an empty, brown beer bottle, wash it thoroughly, and fill it with the cold water that I usually drink when I preach. I reached down to take a drink from that brown beer bottle as I was preaching, and the mixed expressions of shock in the congregation were priceless. Eventually I explained what I was doing to make a point. Many people claim all that matters is who you are on the inside. Well, all that mattered was that there was clean water on the inside of that bottle. But I could have caused someone to stumble if I had not explained the outer appearance of the beer bottle. I never want my "good to be evil spoken of."[1] I'm convinced that when Jesus is truly filling you on the inside, it affects the outside as well. We shouldn't walk around looking and acting just like the world—that is without Jesus—hoping someone notices that He dwells in us. If Jesus is genuinely on the inside, He will be reflected on the outside. It is time to live inside out!

Upside Down Inside Out

In Acts 17, the Greeks were frantically looking for Paul and Silas to do them harm and throw them out of the city. When they couldn't find those two, they took a man named Jason, with whom Paul and Silas had stayed, and accused him of wrongdoing, saying, "These who have turned the world upside down have come here too" (v. 6). We will never turn the world upside down until the body of Christ consistently lives inside out. I am not impressed with how much people shout, how spiritual they act, or how big their Bibles may be. I want to know what is on the inside. That is who you really are. It is like the iceberg that sank the *Titanic*. Only about 20 percent of an iceberg is the part you can see above water. About 80 percent of an iceberg remains hidden under water. What is hidden in your private life matters to God. Your character—the person you are when no one else is looking—matters to God. Your integrity and purity matter to God. Who are you on the inside?

The longer I serve the Lord and the more I do what He has called me to do—the more I need to do a "gut check." Fasting is my gut check. I want to be open like David and look deep inside at the motives in my life. I want to ask myself, "Am I doing it for vainglory? Am I doing it because I'm an ambitious person?" Paul actually talked about missing the mark, about running only to find out that he lost the race.

> Do you not know that those who run in a race all run, but one receives the prize? Run in such a way that you may obtain it. And everyone who competes for the prize is temperate in all things. Now they do it to obtain a perishable crown, but we for an imperishable crown. Therefore I run thus: not with uncertainty. Thus I fight: not as one who beats the air. But I discipline my body and bring it into subjection, lest, when I have preached to others, I myself should become disqualified.
>
> —1 CORINTHIANS 9:24–27

That is why I check myself on a regular basis by fasting regularly. Fasting is self-humbling! Fasting brings you to that place of saying, "Lord, create in me a clean heart. I want to bring You glory. I want to be a vessel You can use." I don't want to just be a preacher who gets up and presents a big, shiny front. I want something inside of me that connects with people. I don't want to talk to heads and tickle itching ears. I want to speak the piercing Word of God to hearts that need more of Jesus.

Out of the Closet

There are two places Jesus tells the church to go: to the lost,[2] and to their closet to pray.[3] The problem is, to a large degree the church has gone into the closet and has never come out! You cannot run a race in your closet. You cannot reach the lost in your closet. The word *church* in the Greek language is *ecclesia*, which means "the called-out ones." We are called to come out of the closet! The Holy Spirit does not come to isolate you from the world. He comes to insulate you from the world. There's a difference between being isolated and insulated. Noah insulated the ark. He applied a thick layer of pitch over the wood to seal it and make it waterproof. The Bible says you have been covered by the blood of Christ and sealed with the Holy Spirit.[4]

We need to live from the inside out as individuals and as the people of God. We need to fast and pray until we get a true burden for souls. There are people with whom you come into contact every day who are going through hell now and will spend eternity there if someone doesn't get a burden to see them saved. People ask what I fast and pray about. Sometimes I pray for a greater burden for souls. Having a burden for something affects the way you live. It forces you out of your comfort zone. When you have a burden on the inside, it shows on the outside.

Churches tend to have the old Pizza Hut mentality. At

one time Pizza Hut was the number one pizza restaurant. But you had to go there to get the pizza because they didn't deliver. They believed their product was superior and people would come in if they wanted it. Then they got knocked out of their spot by lesser quality pizza restaurants that *only* deliver. The competition understood that you have to get the pizza to where the people are located.

Jesus said we would be "fishers of men." How ridiculous would it look for a man to go out into the middle of a lake with a fancy new bass boat and a sign that reads, "Fish Welcome Here"? Those fish are not going to jump into the big shiny boat on their own just because he is sitting there holding a sign. Why then do churches today seem to think that evangelism is an option, that we can just build the building and create the program "and they will come," like the movie *Field of Dreams*? That is not what Jesus had in mind.

We do need time to get alone in our "closet" with God. We need to set aside time for prayer and fasting to sharpen our ax and get the edge back. But then we need to come out SWINGING! When you have a burden on the inside, it changes the way you live on the outside. You start to think about the fact that in one hundred years, everybody you know will be in heaven or hell. You don't get casual when you carry a burden. It's like there is something nudging you to be His witness, to be a light. God didn't save you just so you could go to church one day a week and sing and shout with other saints and then put your faith back in the closet. He equips and empowers us to go out into the world and live inside out.

As a child of God, you are like one of those glow sticks. You have something powerful inside—a light to those locked in darkness. But a glow stick won't shed any of that light as long as it is undisturbed. It has to be bent and broken for the light to be activated. God is bending you and breaking you. But it is in the bending and breaking that you begin to come out of the closet. And when you do, people can see you through your suffering and through your tears. They see the real you going through the same difficulties they face—only with different results. In your breaking and bending, you are sharing the light of the world. They see Jesus in your pain. They see Jesus in your breaking. They feel Jesus in your compassion and in your selflessness.

Chapter 11

Extreme Makeover

W hat does fasting have to do with a makeover? Everything. God said to Samuel, "For the LORD does not see as man sees; for man looks at the outward appearance, but the LORD looks at the heart" (1 Sam. 16:7). It doesn't matter to God how good things appear to be going on the outside if we remain empty, void of His presence on the inside. Fasting cuts through all the junk. Fasting opens the door for the Holy Spirit to come in and do surgery on those weak, withered areas of your spiritual life, replacing them with life and power.

Society pressures us to achieve its "ideal" image of beauty, which has given rise over the years to dozens of different "reality" TV programs designed to turn the so-called ugly ducklings of the world into "swans." Shows like *The Biggest Loser* and *Extreme Makeover: Weight Loss Edition* chronicle the lives of extremely obese individuals as they work to lose nearly half of their body weight.

On the TLC show *What Not to Wear*, the hosts "help the frumpy by giving them life-changing fashion makeovers and fashion advice."[1] A short-lived show titled *The Swan* went to the extreme, taking people who believed they were hopelessly ugly and totally remaking them with life coaches, therapists, intense dental procedures, and cosmetic plastic surgeries. The field of cosmetic plastic surgery continues to grow as the demand for surgical and nonsurgical procedures is ever increasing. Face lifts, tummy tucks, liposuction…it is amazing what doctors can slice off and then stuff, stitch, or inject somewhere else in order to give us the latest "fad" look. For people who have suffered a massive scarring from cancer or a disfiguring injury or malady, reconstructive surgery is a huge blessing for their self-esteem. But the truth is, all of us have looked into a mirror at one time or another and quietly thought about something we would like to change about our outer appearance. It sounds something like, "I wish I could do something about my nose…my eyes look baggy…my wrinkles are increasing…I wish I could take some of this and put it up here…or move some of this down there…if I just could pull this back and lift this up…I would feel much better."

With all the focus on enhancing the outward appearance to meet with the world's ever-changing standard, I think we are missing something. We are overlooking the simple goals of God's heart. As David wrote in Psalm 149,

"For the Lord takes pleasure in His people; He will beautify the humble with salvation" (v. 4). That is what fasting has to do with makeovers.

What we desire to do on the outside reflects what is going on in the heart. When we don't feel that we measure up in our appearance, it drains our confidence. One of the themes threaded throughout these pages is found in the Book of Hebrews: "Therefore do not cast away your confidence, which has great reward. For you have need of endurance, so that after you have done the will of God, you may receive the promise" (Heb. 10:35–36). Satan would like nothing more than to get us to quit the race by stealing our confidence.

Ever since the fall of man in the Garden of Eden, mankind has been in need of a makeover. There were no worries prior to sin entering into the heart of man. Adam and Eve were naked before each other and before God—with no concern regarding their appearance. The first thing they did after sin entered the picture was to attempt to cover their nakedness with leaves. Sin has a way of making us all feel *ugly*. Sin robs us of our confidence and destroys our self-esteem. Sin, no matter how seemingly small, will find a way to make you loathe yourself eventually. When you are bound, addicted, and living in sin, you add the weight of guilt to your appearance. When you don't like who you are, you only see the negative parts of your life. God sees who you are and who He has planned for you to become.

Master Surgeon

How is it that we will run to a doctor and show him or her all of our "unbecoming" parts, expecting a miracle—but we hesitate to come to God the Creator, the master surgeon, to show Him the weak and withered parts of our spirit? A typical plastic surgeon keeps an album of his or her success stories, usually including the "before and after" shots. You can look at a book or a computer screen and request the nose of that "famous person," another's cheekbones, someone else's chin, ears, front side, or backside! Well, God has a book too. He can empower you to overcome any addiction, be it drugs, alcohol, homosexuality, sexual addictions, pornography, overeating, etc. He can deliver you from the bonds of sin and death and give you everlasting life. He can take your cold, stony heart and give you a heart of flesh. He can put His Word and His ways in your heart so that you will walk according to the Spirit and not fulfill the lust of the flesh. Who are some of His clients?

How about Jacob, who was known as a deceiver? He was a con artist. His name means "worm." By the time God got through with him, Jacob went from being a worm to being a prince. God so transformed him that he became a patriarch of saints.

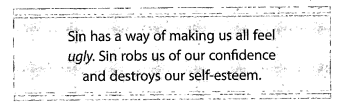

Sin has a way of making us all feel *ugly*. Sin robs us of our confidence and destroys our self-esteem.

Remember the Samaritan woman at the well whom we talked about earlier? Jesus helped her remove the mask she had been living behind, pretending to be something that she wasn't. Jesus gave her a "faith lift" and got down to the core of who she was created to be, a woman who worshiped God freely in spirit and in truth. We serve a God who can do reconstructive surgery on your entire life—past, present, and future!

One fine Sabbath day Jesus found a man in need of an extreme makeover in the synagogue. The Pharisees questioned Jesus as to whether it was lawful to heal on the Sabbath, trying to ensnare Him. Jesus answered their question with a question:

> "What man is there among you who has one sheep, and if it falls into a pit on the Sabbath, will not lay hold of it and lift it out? Of how much more value then is a man than a sheep? Therefore it is lawful to do good on the Sabbath." Then He said to the man, "Stretch out your hand." And he stretched it out, and it was restored as whole as the other.
>
> —MATTHEW 12:11–13

The man was crippled in his hand, but it affected his entire perspective on life. That hand most likely limited his work and, therefore, his place in society. It is reasonable to assume that the man's confidence was gone and his self-image was lowered due to his physical limitation. The Pharisees were content to leave him in that condition in order to make their point. They were more concerned with *being* right than they were in *doing* what was right.

When Jesus spoke to the man, notice that He didn't say, "Stretch out your withered hand." He did not focus on the man's limitations but on his possibilities. Jesus said, "Stretch out your hand." Most of us would have stretched out our good hand! We don't want to present the withered parts of our life. We want to hide our weaknesses—the very things God seeks to touch. That is not how Jesus approaches us. He sees. He knows. He offers an "extreme makeover" when we are willing to show Him our weaknesses, the withered parts of our life that we don't want anyone else to see.

The show *Extreme Makeover: Home Edition* has people submit video applications to request a makeover of their current residence. The stories they feature on the show truly tug at your heartstrings. Many have specific handicaps or are families that take in a multitude of orphaned children or serve their community in an amazing way. In the application process, they have to video the limitations of their homes. They have to show the holey, leaking roof.

They have to expose where the foundation is crumbling, where the plumbing doesn't work, where the rodents run through, where their kids all sleep on one mattress on the floor, and where the house is just falling down around them.

Get to the Root—Fast!

What concerns me is the number of Christians who would put faith in the process of applying for a home makeover or even a physical makeover—but still will not take the time to fast and pray, exposing the limitations, weaknesses, and withered areas of their lives to the Lord for His makeover. The man in the synagogue made the right decision. He didn't pretend everything was fine in front of the religious crowd. He stretched out the area that he needed God to touch. When he did, Jesus gave him an extreme makeover, healing him instantly.

Don't ever hesitate to show God your problem. When you declare a fast, you are effectively saying, "Jesus, I am going to show You the withered parts of my life. I am going to show You the messed-up areas of my marriage, my relationships, and my family. I'm going to show You my hurts, my wounded areas that haven't healed yet— and I'm going to trust You to get to the root of things and bring healing to those areas. Lord, I need an extreme makeover!"

An added benefit to fasting starts once you have finished showing God what you know to be your problem areas. Then He takes over. When you start to fast, the Holy Spirit has access to bring up every ugly thing in your life that needs attention. If you have a temper, it will surface on a fast. If you have unforgiveness, it will come to the surface. Things you may not even know were affecting your walk with God will come to the surface. Your job is to trust God to get it *all* out.

The man from Gadara hid nothing from Jesus. Once a citizen of that city, somehow he had become possessed by demons and was living in the graveyard. Once an average guy doing a normal job, he had started running around without clothes, cutting himself with sharp stones. He had even been placed under guard and bound with chains, but he broke free like a wild man. No one could or would get near him. No one but Jesus, that is. No matter what you think is too disgusting for Jesus to see—He already knows about it and is able to help. That tormented, dangerous man was deeply scarred. Whatever possesses you will mark you. If you are possessed by the world, the world will mark you. But Jesus will change you. He cast the demons out of the man. He restored the man's mind, and I imagine the disciples helped him find some clothes. When the town's people came to see what happened, they were frightened by the man's complete and total transformation. He had gone from being a wild beast to a man whole, healed, dressed, and in his right mind. Jesus sent him out to tell everyone his testimony of God's extreme makeover.[2]

His makeover was so radical that people from town could hardly believe it was the same man. It reminds me of when the staff of a New York talk show will grab some unsuspecting tourist off the street and totally make them over. They intentionally look for folks who are a total mess with crazy hair, outdated clothing, and a worn-out expression. They take them back stage, and experts begin restyling the hair and applying new makeup and a new wardrobe. A few hours later their "victim" emerges, and the audience can't believe it is the same person. Even more shocked are the person's family and spouse.

As dramatic as all that is—it doesn't remotely compare to what Jesus does in your life! And His work is ongoing. Paul said, "Therefore if any person is [ingrafted] in Christ (the Messiah) he is a new creation (a new creature altogether); the old [previous moral and spiritual condition] has passed away. Behold, the fresh and new has come!" (2 Cor. 5:17, AMP). The man from Gadara had scars from everything that the devil had done to destroy his life. The good news is that Jesus uses people with scars. Jesus uses people who have a "past." When you bring your scars and issues to Him, He will give you a makeover, giving you beauty for ashes, strength for scars, and His grace to cover your weakness.

When He begins to make over your life, it is time to clean out the closet and get rid of the frumpy spiritual attire. Just like people who still wear "mom jeans" decades after the fad has faded, some Christians still adorn themselves in outdated spiritual attire. People wake up, walk to the closet, and start layering on what they are comfortable wearing. Most of the time it starts with a layer of past hurts and rejection. It's broken in really well and goes with everything, woven with threads of hurt from family, friends, people from work—everyone. And what goes better with hurt and rejection than a stylish layer of guilt from your past? It is a little heavy, but it works for just about every season. And nothing pulls the whole outfit together better than a touch of worthlessness, fear, depression, and worry. That stuff just doesn't fit when you are a new creation in Christ. You need to put on a layer of thankfulness and joy in the Lord. You need the garment of praise for the spirit of heaviness.[3] How about some grace in your spiritual closet to cover you every day, wherever you go? It covers a lot of imperfections!

That is what the prodigal son found when he returned home—grace. He came dragging back, hoping for nothing more than to be as a servant in his father's house. His past actions assured him that he did not deserve to be considered a son ever again. He was covered in filth and disgrace, shame and guilt. But his father had been watching for him. Jesus said, "When he was still a great way off, his father saw him and had compassion, and ran and fell on his neck and kissed him" (Luke 15:20). The father then had his servants bring out the best robe, shoes for his feet, and a ring to put on his hand that indicated his family status.[4] When you are a child of the King, He expects you to dress like you belong to Him. Remember, the Lord takes pleasure in you!

Catalog of Faith

What if you could select a greater level of faith the same way you would select a new nose or chin at a plastic surgeon's office? You could point to the faith of Joshua, who led the people of Israel into the Promised Land, saw the walls of Jericho fall according to God's instruction, and even commanded the sun to stand still so he could finish a battle one day.[5] You could point to Peter's anointing for healing the sick with nothing but the passing of his shadow and say, "Lord, I desire an anointing like that." Or you could go for the *ultimate package* and say, "I want to be like Jesus."

I want you to understand that you *should* desire greater faith and greater anointing. Paul said we should "earnestly desire the best gifts" (1 Cor. 12:31). There's just one thing to keep in mind: there are no shortcuts. You won't get there with a dull ax! You need the edge that fasting gives you. The people in God's Word who were commended for having great faith had committed themselves to a high standard. They weren't benchwarmers, or in this case, pew warmers.

Fasting is not a requirement; it is a choice. It is a vow you choose to make to pursue God on a deeper level. The entire time that you are on a fast you are acknowledging God. When you are feeling hungry, empty, and weak, you connect with God without all the clutter. In that way fasting is a time vow. It is also a discipline vow. Fasting, especially a longer fast, strengthens your character in every area of your life. Staying disciplined throughout a lengthy fast strengthens you in other areas in which you may have grown lax or comfortable—even frumpy! A lengthy fast strengthens your will. It strengthens your inner man. Like sharpening your ax for the work or battle of life, it helps you live in purity and holiness before God. Fasting helps you discipline your body to glorify God.

> When you bring your scars and issues to Him, He will give you a makeover, giving you beauty for ashes, strength for scars, and His grace to cover your weakness.

Fasting allows you to lay your life on the master surgeon's table to have negative, deadly things cut away. He can replace them with healthy, beautiful, life-giving characteristics. You wouldn't get up off of a plastic surgeon's table halfway through surgery and yell, "I quit. I'll take half a nose and just leave the other half hanging!" Likewise you never want to cut a fast short and quit before the God the Surgeon is finished. A side benefit of a lengthy fast is that it gives God time to root out the sin in your life and bring it to the surface so that you can be truly free.

Come Away

The more Jesus healed, the more the crowds followed Him. Luke recorded, "But so much the more the news spread abroad concerning Him, and great crowds kept coming together to hear [Him] and to be healed by Him of their infirmities. But He Himself withdrew [in retirement] to the wilderness (desert) and prayed" (Luke 5:15–16, AMP). Jesus knew how important it was to "come away" and be with God in prayer. When you fast, it is a season to come away, to set yourself apart from the routine of life, the business, the mindless entertainment and to sink deeply into God's Word. When you are empty, quiet, and broken before Him, you can hear His voice more clearly. I was on a TV program one night with Pastor Larry Stockstill.

He was on a total fast at the time, and he talked about his "fasting trailer." He has a simple little trailer out in the country where he can get away for a day or two and fast. It has no television, no radio, no Internet. He loves to go to that trailer to just lock himself away with Jesus for a while.

Jesus invites you to come away and be persistent. Another value in an extended fast is the persistence it represents. Jesus told a few stories about persistent people and how their persistence alone got them what they desired. He said, "Men always ought to pray and not lose heart" (Luke 18:1). One story is about a man waking his neighbor for bread. He knocked and knocked until his neighbor finally gave him the bread to make him go away.[6] He told another story of a persistent widow who demanded justice in a legal situation.[7] Jesus also met a Gentile woman who persistently asked Him to heal her daughter. She would not take no for an answer. He commended the woman's faith, and her daughter was healed.[8] Fasting is persistent prayer. Keep asking, keep seeking, keep knocking!

Tear It Down to Build It Up

On the TV show *Extreme Makeover: Home Edition*, once the crew has inspected the house and figured out just how bad the situation looks, they move on to the next step—demolition. One of the highlights of each program is sending the family live footage of their house being totally demolished while they are away on a fantastic vacation. Fasting has a way of doing that in your spiritual life. Fasting gives the Holy Spirit a sledge hammer and a bulldozer to come in and tear down the broken walls, the sagging foundations, the leaking roof—and start fresh with a firm foundation. It is a process called brokenness.

Someone once said, "If your eyes are always dry, it means your soul is dry." Genuine brokenness is often accompanied by weeping. Even during a six-day fast for her family, my sister experienced weeping that lasted for a day or two past the end of the fast. It was an outward expression of a deep, intimate work of the Holy Spirit. I realize that some people are very uncomfortable with emotional release. But consider it part of the makeover! Weeping is a natural side effect of true fasting. It is often the evidence that God is breaking you so that He can rebuild you. If you feel His presence working in you and tears begin to come up, let them flow because tears are powerful. Tears are cleansing. Tears unto the Lord are a form of worship. And there's something about weeping and fasting that gets God's attention. God said through the prophet Joel, "Turn and keep on coming to Me with all your heart, with fasting, with weeping, and with mourning [until every hindrance is removed and the broken fellowship is restored]. Rend your hearts and not your garments and return to the Lord, your God, for He is gracious and merciful, slow to anger, and abounding in loving-kindness; and He revokes His sentence of evil [when His conditions are met]" (Joel 2:12–13, AMP).

Extreme Transformation

A retired player for the Atlanta Braves recently gave his testimony one Sunday. He had been in the major leagues for about fourteen years when he retired. But he had been hooked on chewing tobacco for twenty-three years. He wanted to quit and had tried many times. He was involved in his church and had a passion for youth ministry, but he didn't feel like he could fully be used because of the power the addiction had over his life. His wife encouraged him to join our annual twenty-one-day fast in January. He had never fasted before and was honest enough to admit that he really didn't want to start. But he decided to try anyway.

On the third day of the fast he stopped for gas and bought five cans of tobacco. As he was walking out of the store, he felt like he heard God speak to his heart for the first time in his life. The words were simple and to the point: "Throw it away, and you'll never want it again." He continued walking, got in his car, and pulled onto the highway. As he drove, he began to talk to God. He said, "Lord, I have tried this so many times, and it just doesn't work." He had traveled about a mile when God spoke to him again: "Throw it away, and you'll never want it again." There was no mistaking the door of opportunity that the Holy Spirit was swinging open for him. He drove home and immediately threw all five unopened cans of tobacco in the trash can. From that moment on, true to God's word, *he has never wanted it again!*

Sometimes the thing that prevents God from having His way in our lives is simply what is locked between our ears. Just as we do with old wardrobes, we tend to hold on to old ways of thinking, old patterns, old failures. The enemy had convinced this retired ballplayer that he would never be free from chewing tobacco, that he was too weak to overcome it in his own power. When we stop trying to do things all in our own power and instead choose to humble ourselves before God and trust Him to make over our weaknesses, the lies of the enemy lose their power! As the apostle Paul said:

> I beseech you therefore, brethren, by the mercies of God, that you present your bodies a living sacrifice, holy, acceptable to God, which is your reasonable service. And do not be conformed to this world, but be transformed by the renewing of your mind, that you may prove what is that good and acceptable and perfect will of God.
>
> —ROMANS 12:1–2

I was blessed to have the opportunity to meet with Elmer Towns, who helped establish Liberty University several years ago with Dr. Jerry Falwell. Liberty University has become this country's largest private, nonprofit university. But in the early days there were times that, without serious fasting and prayer, it may not have made it. The way Dr. Falwell would call the school to seasons of fasting and prayer in the face of a serious need inspired Towns, especially when he saw God meet those needs. He had read about fasting in the Word of God, but he had not made it a practice until he experienced God's faithful provision for that school. When he and his wife relocated from Chicago to Virginia, they were faced with two mortgage payments because their Chicago home had not sold. The market was down and prospects were slim. In his book *The Beginner's Guide to Fasting,* Towns shares the story of how fasting affected the sale of their house:

> I asked my wife to fast and pray with me on the fifteenth day of the month, because that was the date the Chicago payment was due. We fasted and prayed that month but the house didn't sell. I forgot about fasting until the fifteenth day of the following month , but then again it didn't sell.
>
> After fasting and praying the third month, the Realtor phoned to say there was finally a nibble. In a down real estate market, only one person looked at my house, but he returned several

times to check out details. We finally closed the sale almost one year after we first fasted. At the closing, the buyer told me he began looking at my house on his wife's birthday, the day after Ruth and I had fasted the very first time. I learned two things from that experience: First, fasting takes prayer to a higher level of fulfillment, and second, don't quit too soon.[9]

It took time, but they did not quit. They continued to trust God for His provision, and that experience helped to transform their understanding of fasting. God honored the power of persistence in fasting and prayer.

Now...it's time for your extreme makeover!

Chapter 12

The Quit Option

One thing that I tell people who are in the midst of severe trials is—never *ever* allow yourself to make permanent decisions based on temporary circumstances. Have you felt like giving up and just throwing in the towel? Maybe you have grown tired of all the battles and struggles. You thought living for Jesus would mean life would be rosy and rainbows, but the continued disappointments have caused your hope to fade. I understand that. What is more important is the fact that Jesus understands it too. Don't forget that He was tempted to take shortcuts and quit when He was fasting in the desert for forty days. In the garden praying, Jesus could have just said, "It's too much, Father. I know it's Your will, but it's just too much." At His arrest, Jesus said He could have called upon twelve legions of angels to defend Him.[1] Yet He pressed on. He did not quit. The number one thing the enemy would like to get us to do is to quit. It may be quitting your marriage, quitting your dream, or even quitting your walk with the Lord. You could decide to quit fighting your flesh, your battle with an addiction or some other sin, and just give in to temptation instead.

When you think about quitting, then you begin to talk about quitting. When you talk about quitting, be assured that, eventually, you will quit. I'm here to tell you that you don't have to quit! You *can* find a place of strengthening in the Lord, just like Elijah and all of the other men and women whom God has used for His glory. As Hebrews 10:39 says, "We are not of those who draw back to perdition, but of those who believe to the saving of the soul."

That is why I believe so strongly in the power of fasting as a regular discipline in every believer's life. Fasting gives you the opportunity to come away from the bombardment of life's difficulties and disappointments in order to hear more clearly from the Lord. When you fast, it is much easier for you to get God's perspective on your circumstances and find His path through the storm. He wants to strengthen your mind, your heart, and your spirit. The Bible instructs us to set our minds on things above for a reason.[2] What you think about is what you will talk about. When you talk faith, you empower faith. When you talk doubt, you empower doubt. When you set your mind on things above, you set your mind on Christ and His example. And Jesus never quit. I want to give you some powerful insights on "removing the quit option," because when you truly set your mind on a goal, quitting is no longer an option.

SEAL Training

When I started reading the book *Lone Survivor*, written by Navy SEAL Marcus Luttrell, I couldn't put it down.[3] The Lord used that book to ignite in my spirit a fresh commitment to *never quit*. The Navy SEALs are among our most elite fighting forces. The acronym SEAL is a reminder that they are fully trained to get the job done with stealth and precision at sea, in the air, and on land. On May 2, 2011, headlines around the world announced the death of al Qaeda leader Osama bin Laden, the man responsible for planning the worst terror attack on US soil. He was killed when US Navy SEAL Team 6 successfully raided his compound in Abbottabad, Pakistan. Luttrell's team was in Afghanistan in 2005, involved in what became the deadliest day in the history of the SEALs.

In his book Luttrell recounts the unbelievably strenuous training process required to become a SEAL. Luttrell is a Texas man, with a rugged zest for life from his childhood. He set his goal to become a Navy SEAL by the time he was twelve years old and soon after enrolled himself in the rigorous pretraining provided by Sergeant Shelton, a local hero who served as a Green Beret in Vietnam. Shelton told

Luttrell and the others in training, "I'm gonna break you down, mentally and physically....Then I'm gonna build you right back up, as one fighting unit—so your mind and body are one."[4] The whole time I was reading this book I couldn't help but think of the many connections there were to fasting. That is what fasting does—it breaks you down and breaks you out of the worldly ruts and routines so that you can be built back up in the strength and power of the Holy Spirit.

> When you fast, it is much easier for you to get God's perspective on your circumstances and find His path through the storm.

Luttrell made it through Shelton and boot camp and shipped off to the Navy amphibious base on Coronado Island. There he faced two weeks of indoctrination before even starting BUD/S training (Basic Underwater Demolition/SEALs). Surprisingly, the first thing they were taught in "Indoc" was not how to blow up stuff underwater. The first thing that was drilled into their heads was the concept of a swim buddy. In the SEALs, you never leave a man behind, dead or alive. So the very first major instruction you receive is to never be more than an arm's length away from your "swim buddy," no matter where you go. He's your teammate, and you never separate for any reason. I wish the body of Christ could take a course in that sometimes. How different things might be if we could all have that same credo—never ever leave anyone behind. I always say that fasting with a friend is so powerful because you have someone else who is going through what you are going through. You can share what God is showing you and come out on the other side changed. Considering the rest of the training that these men undergo, it is profound that this is the first thing they are taught.

Those two weeks in "Indoc" usually whittle away a few of the men who do not have what it takes to go forward. But those who survive begin BUD/S, a seven-month program where the real rubber meets the road and where, according to Luttrell, SEAL instructors drive men to within an inch of their lives. There's no way that I can detail all of what they endure here. Immediately after wake-up call at four in the morning they dash into ice-cold pressurized water jets for showers, then off to hundreds of push-ups, sit-ups, and flutter kicks in and out of training drills. They were repeatedly told to get "wet and sandy," jumping into the cold ocean water and then rolling around in the sand—and *then* continuing whatever grueling exercise they were carrying out. Luttrell once counted 450 push-ups before breakfast! The instructors set up scenes of total chaos to break the men down. They were drilled carrying logs overhead while running through water. They carried their boats out to sea and back again and ran four miles in sand in less than thirty-two minutes, sometimes several times a day. And that's before breakfast! Just when it seemed like they were getting in condition, the instructors would raise the bar higher, adding more chaos and more grueling training. The instructors sometimes called for room inspection and then ransacked the rooms so that everyone failed inspection. Luttrell writes that the instructors watched man after man "DOR," which stands for Drop On Request, and leave the program. He said, "They were only interested in the others, the ones who did not crack or quit. The ones who would rather die than quit. The ones with no quit in them."[5]

There was a procedure for quitting. When you'd had enough, when you had come to believe that you truly could not take any more, you could exercise your quit option by walking to the office, laying down your helmet, and ringing the big bell by the door. You would be shipped back to whatever rank you had prior to attempting to become a SEAL. The instructors made it clear that there was no shame in quitting. They tell the men from the beginning that two-thirds will quit before it's over. And it isn't over until Hell Week is over.

Hell Week is legendary in the BUD/S. It starts about five weeks into the program, late one Sunday afternoon and ends on Friday. Those who make it through are so beat down, worn out, sleep deprived, and totally exhausted by the time it ends, some don't even know what day of the week it is. It starts with casual clothes, stacks of pizza and movies, and then "it" breaks out with rapid gunfire from all sides, whistles blowing, doors crashing down, high-pressure water jets, explosions, and total chaos. Without time to think, the men are under one long surprise attack intended to simulate the Normandy beaches that continues all week long. They are worked around the clock in intense calisthenics, training drills, water drills, and worse. They are in and out of 60 degree water, sometimes staying as long as fifteen to twenty minutes, nearly long enough for hypothermia to set in, but not quite. Of some of the men who quit during Hell Week, Luttrell noticed that, "They had allowed themselves to live in dread of the pain and anguish to come."[6] Their commanding officer had warned the men to focus on completing each task as it came and live for that day. Those who did not heed his words gave up. Those who took the advice of their leader—who had been through all this before them—who fixed their minds on completing the task at hand continued on. I think about the power in the words of Hebrews:

> Therefore we also, since we are surrounded by so great a cloud of witnesses, let us lay aside every weight, and the sin which so easily ensnares us, and let us run with endurance the race that is set before us, looking unto Jesus, the author and

finisher of our faith, who for the joy that was set before Him endured the cross, despising the shame, and has sat down at the right hand of the throne of God.

—Hebrews 12:1–2

These men had been trained for weeks physically and mentally—to endure. They were taught how to take care of their bodies so that when the heat was really on, their bodies could take care of them. What Hell Week was designed to do was break down the mind. Up to that point, Luttrell says the men had been told "the real battle is won in the mind. It's won by guys who understand their areas of weakness, who sit and think about it, plotting and planning to improve. Attending to the detail. Work on their weaknesses and overcome them. Because they can."[7] I've said from the beginning of this book that God isn't as interested in our strengths as He is interested in our weaknesses. When we can learn to bring those things to the front, He will teach us how to overcome those things in His strength.

Luttrell saw many men leave the program, but the ones who left during Hell Week left a greater impression. One drill had them doing flutter kicks with their heads and shoulders in the ocean. Even though they had done them before, that day it was the trigger for two more men to quit. During Hell Week, the instructors would ask the men if they were sure, giving them another chance before they rang the bell. One of the men wavered but chose to quit that day. Luttrell said, "I later learned that when a man quits and is given another chance and takes it, he never makes it through. All the instructors know that. If the thought of DOR enters a man's head, he is not a Navy SEAL."[8]

That is powerful. If the thought of dropping on request, of quitting, enters your mind, you're not a Navy SEAL. How many failed marriages could have been prevented if the couple entered into that covenant agreement with the understanding that, "If the thought of leaving, adultery, pornography addiction, or divorce is an option in your mind—you aren't a husband...you aren't a wife." Are you a Christian with a quit option? Jesus said, "No one, having put his hand to the plow, and looking back, is fit for the kingdom of God" (Luke 9:62). No matter what it is in this life, if the option to quit and give up is available, once you decide that is an option, you will take that option when circumstances get tough enough. We need to understand that we are in a battle and our enemy is going to throw everything he can at us to discourage us, break us down, and get us to quit pursuing the King of kings with all our heart, mind, soul, and strength.

Where the Battle Must Be Won First

Just like many who quit in Luttrell's training group, who blamed their decision to quit on the torturous training, the cold water, or unfair treatment—we need to understand that the battle is not about what we're facing. The battle is not with your family or marriage, a financial problem, or an illness. The battle that must be won first is in your thinking. The devil desires to break down your mind. He wants to break you down mentally, to cause you to give up, to quit, to say, "I can't take it anymore. I'm going to use my quit option. I'm going to ring the bell and go back to how things used to be." You get to the point where you believe you have no more energy to fight and no ability to overcome. I'm here to remind you that you are more than conquerors in Christ Jesus, in His strength. But the only way that will become a reality in your life is if you remove the quit option. When you do that—the real battle is already won.

> Are you a Christian with a quit option?

The writer of the Book of Hebrews said, "Therefore do not cast away your confidence, which has great reward. For you have need of endurance, so that after you have done the will of God, you may receive the promise" (Heb.

10:35–36). We have need of endurance! Just like those enrolled in SEAL team training who had to endure the grueling physical and mental strain in order to receive SEAL status, we need to endure the battles and overcome so that we may receive the promise of God. "We are not of those who draw back to perdition, but of those who believe to the saving of the soul" (v. 39). We do not draw back! I love that scripture because so many really do start out strong. They start out on fire for God, but somewhere along the way they enter into their own Hell Week, and trouble starts breaking loose on every front. That's when they start looking for the bell to ring, because they never got rid of that option before they started. It doesn't matter how strong you start if quitting is always an option.

I don't care what the enemy throws at me; I have made up my mind that I am not turning back. I am not of those who draw back, and I don't believe you are either. There is no quit option. I have had prayers answered, and I've had prayers go unanswered. I have had miracles happen, and I've endured huge disappointments. I've had high mountains where God gave me things and amazed me in awesome ways, and I've had low, low valleys where I felt God-forsaken and cried all night long. But I am not in this for what I can get out of Jesus. I'm in this because He loved me first and gave Himself for me. When I will recognize my weakness and trust in His strength, He will give me the mercy and grace to endure. "Let us therefore come boldly to the throne of grace, that we may obtain mercy and find grace to help in time of need" (Heb. 4:16).

However—and this is important—if the Lord were to never answer another prayer, I will *still* never ring that bell. As Job said, "Though He slay me, yet will I trust Him" (Job 13:15). Job had thrown away the quit option. The three friends of Daniel—Shadrach, Meshach, and Abed-Nego—had thrown away the quit option. They told King Nebuchadnezzar, "Our God whom we serve is able to deliver us from the burning fiery furnace, and He will deliver us from your hand, O king. But if not, let it be known to you, O king, that we do not serve your gods, nor will we worship the gold image which you have set up" (Dan. 3:17–18). They maintained their confidence in God's ability to deliver them, and even more, they had eliminated the quit option. Even if God *didn't* choose to deliver them from the fiery furnace, they would still not bow the knee to Nebuchadnezzar's idols.

More Than Conquerors

There is no quit option in my emergency plan, and there should not be one in yours either. I have nothing to go back to. My worst day with Jesus is better than my best day in the world without God! I crossed that bridge a long time ago. The enemy, this world, difficult circumstances—

it doesn't matter. I'll still be in church. I'll still lift my hands in worship. I'll still worship Him with my tithe. I'll still serve Him with all I have. I do not have a quit option in my mind anymore. Thank You, Lord, for the power of a made-up mind!

I am never going to ring that bell. I am never going to walk away from God. I am never going to quit church. I am never going to leave my wife. I am never going to give up on my kids. I am never going to let my dream die. I am never going to quit preaching. I am never going to quit living for Jesus. This needs to get deep in your spirit. While preaching in Corinth, Paul went into a detailed discourse of some of the things he had encountered and endured after coming to Jesus. He had served the Lord with tears, in chains, against temptations and false accusations, and evading those who wanted him dead:

> ...in labors more abundant, in stripes above measure, in prisons more frequently, in deaths often. From the Jews five times I received forty stripes minus one. Three times I was beaten with rods; once I was stoned; three times I was shipwrecked; a night and a day I have been in the deep; in journeys often, in perils of waters, in perils of robbers, in perils of my own countrymen, in perils of the Gentiles, in perils in the city, in perils in the wilderness, in perils in the sea, in perils among false brethren; in weariness and

toil, in sleeplessness often, in hunger and thirst, in fastings often, in cold and nakedness—besides the other things, what comes upon me daily: my deep concern for all the churches.

—2 Corinthians 11:23–28

Paul had a made-up mind that he would not only finish the race, but also that he was going to do it with joy! There was no quit option for him. He was bombarded with trials and attacks everywhere he went, but that did not change his resolve, and we cannot allow it to change ours either. If anything, it should make us stronger. As Paul said, "Yet in all these things we are more than conquerors through Him who loved us. For I am persuaded that neither death nor life, nor angels nor principalities nor powers, nor things present nor things to come, nor height nor depth, nor any other created thing, shall be able to separate us from the love of God which is in Christ Jesus our Lord" (Rom. 8:37–39).

Those grueling days of training prepared Luttrell for the real battles that would be faced in combat. In June 2005, he faced a battle like no other. His team had been sent to take out a notorious al Qaeda leader in Afghanistan. He and his three team members were in deep cover on the side of a mountain when they were discovered by local goat herders. They allowed the men to live, knowing that they could be working for the enemy—and they were.

Within no time, the SEAL team was under attack from 150 or more Taliban soldiers out for blood. One by one Luttrell's team was hit. He had taken cover with the one remaining team member when the enemy launched a grenade at the two of them. It blew him halfway down the mountain and filled his leg with shrapnel. When he came to, he realized he was the only one left alive. He took cover again—but never quit. Severely wounded, bleeding profusely, he set his rifle to take out the first enemy he saw. They were hunting for him and closing in.

One of his team had managed a distress call before he died. But when the MH-47 helicopter loaded with other SEAL team members and Special Forces arrived to rescue their men, the Taliban fired a rocket into the helicopter, blowing it up along with the soldiers. The next day, some local tribesmen found Luttrell and took care of his wounds, at risk to their own safety. He was eventually rescued and brought home, the lone survivor of the greatest loss of life in SEAL history.

What I hope you take away from Luttrell's story is the fact that the battle is fought in your mind before it is ever fought openly. If you have determined in your heart that you will endure no matter what—that there is *no* quit option—you will make it through anything. Jesus is our ultimate example. He is the "author and finisher of our faith" (Heb. 12:2). He endured from beginning to end. He never took shortcuts. He never quit. He endured the whip when they beat His back until it looked like ribbons falling from His flesh. He endured the beating, the humiliation, the spit, the accusations, and the soldier's slaps across His face. He endured the nails as they stretched Him across the timbers of the cross and brutally pierced His hands and His feet. He could have quit—but He endured. He was set from the beginning to carry out the will of the Father and redeem fallen man—you and me—no matter what. If He can do that, He can bring you through anything!

Young people, you need to remove the quit option from your life while you are still living under the protective eye of your parents at home. Don't wait until you're on the battlefield to make up your mind. You won't have the strength to endure when you are on your own, in college or some other worldly environment where everybody is partying and drinking, using drugs, and sleeping with five or six people a week. If you haven't already crossed that bridge in your mind and said, "I'll never quit serving Jesus Christ," then you will quit when things get to be too rough. If you haven't removed the quit option before that time, Satan will make sure he puts the temptation and the pressure on you. He knows whether or not you mean it. He knows whether or not you are playing the game or if you are sold out, serving Jesus with all of your heart, mind, soul, and strength.

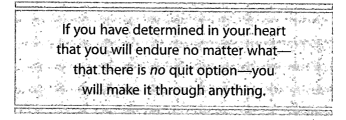

If you have determined in your heart that you will endure no matter what—that there is *no* quit option—you will make it through anything.

Are you fighting addictions? Now is the time to remove the quit option once and for all. Then and only then will you see victory. Without that determination, it is too easy to "ring the bell" and go back to your drugs, alcohol, cigarettes, pornography—whatever it is. But when you can say to the devil, "I may be under more pressure than I've ever been, but I have removed the quit option," you will overcome!

Are you facing difficulties in your marriage? As long as you entertain a quit option in your mind, then there is a chance you will take that option when things get tough enough. You cannot enter a marriage with divorce being an option for hard times or when the "thrill is gone." If that option is still floating around in your thoughts, you need to fast and pray and ask God to give you a fresh start with the grace to remove the quit option from your marriage.

We Need the Fasting Edge

Just like removing the quit option in the early days of SEAL training paid off years later on the field of bloody combat, when you remove the quit option at the beginning of a fast—you are conditioning yourself to succeed beyond the fast. Whether you are going to fast for one day or for forty days, make up your mind that you are going to endure, that you are never going to quit. You will build up more and more endurance, more and more confidence each time. Fasting brings you closer to God. Fasting is "sharpening your ax." Fasting is how you maintain the edge in your life, the edge you need to overcome.

Maybe all of your life you've been a quitter. It is time to remove the quit option once and for all. Our God is a finisher. Paul said, "And I am convinced and sure of this very thing, that He Who began a good work in you will continue until the day of Jesus Christ [right up to the time of His return], developing [that good work] and perfecting and bringing it to full completion in you" (Phil. 1:6, AMP). God will never quit you. He will finish you. But you need remove the quit option from your walk with God. Set aside time as soon as possible to fast and seek Him. Recommit to God and tell Him, "Lord, I am not of those who draw back. I started, and I'm going to finish. With Your help, Lord, I'm removing the quit option from my life. I will not take hold of the plow and look back.

By Your unfailing mercy and grace I will not go back to my old life. I thank You that I was made clean and free through the blood of Jesus, and I will never, never, quit!"

Now, perhaps more than ever, the church needs to get the edge back. Compromise, immorality, indiscretions, and sin have dulled the edge of the power of God—and the church desperately needs to get the edge back. As I said earlier, the people of God are made up of "persons of God." The SEAL training weeded out those individuals who were not serious, who had not removed the quit option, because they would eventually weaken the entire team. When the church gets serious about God's call to "humble themselves, and pray" (2 Chron. 7:14), seeking Him through fasting and repentance, then the church will grow stronger and start seeing the edge return once again.

Notes

Introduction

1. Jentezen Franklin, *Fasting* (Lake Mary, FL: Charisma House, 2008).

2. See Revelation 3:16.

Chapter 1—You Need to Regain the Edge

1. Fasting Movement, http://www.jentezenfranklin.org/fasting.

2. See Hebrews 11:6.

3. Anthony T. Evans, *Tony Evans Speaks Out on Fasting* (Chicago: Moody Publishers, 2000), 5–6.

4. See 2 Kings 2–5.

5. Revelation 1:8.

6. Hebrews 12:2.

7. Dutch Sheets, *God's Timing for Your Life* (Ventura, CA: Regal Books, 2001), 31.

8. 7HillsChurch.tv, "About Pastor Marcus Mecum," http://www.7hillschurch.tv/ImNew/PastorMarcusMecum (accessed July 20, 2011).

9. Nothing in this book is intended to give medical advice.

Chapter 2—The Power of a Made-Up Mind

1. Job 1:13–19.

2. Job 2:6–10.

3. Genesis 22.

4. Genesis 37; 39.

5. Charles W. Henderson, *Marine Sniper: 93 Confirmed Kills* (New York: Berkley Books, 1986) 199–200.

6. John 10:10.

7. Henderson, *Marine Sniper*, 213–215.

8. Ibid., 216.

Chapter 3—Wisdom Brings Success

1. Matthew 3:17.

2. See Genesis 1–3.

3. Hudson Taylor, "The China Inland Mission and the Power of Believing Prayer," in Andrew Murray, *The Key to the Missionary Problem: Thoughts Suggested by the Report of the Ecumenical Missionary Conference on Foreign Missions (1900: New York, N.Y.)* (New York: BiblioLife, LLC, 2009), 96.

4. Ephesians 2:8–10; John 14:12–17.

Chapter 4—The Fast I Have Chosen

1. 1 Samuel 16:1–13.

2. Torie Bosch, "Human Trafficking Awareness Day: Millions Held in Forced Labor, US Says," AOLNews.com, January 11, 2011, http://www .aolnews.com/2011/01/11/human-trafficking-awareness-day-millions-held-in -forced-labor/ (accessed July 21, 2011).

3. UNICEF.org, "Fact Sheet on Commercial Sexual Exploitation and Trafficking of Children," http://www.unicef.org/indonesia/Factsheet_CSEC_ trafficking_Indonesia.pdf (accessed July 21, 2011).

4. Stop Child Trafficking Now, "Child Trafficking Statistics," http://www .sctnow.org/contentpages.aspx?parentnavigationid=5827&viewcontentpage guid=29d295d1-5818-4e7a-bde1-f61690fa44a8 (accessed July 21, 2011).

5. See John 4:1–45.

6. Hudson Taylor, *Hudson Taylor's Choice Sayings: A Compilation from His Writings and Addresses* (London: China Inland Mission, n.d.) 69.

7. Mark 10:46–52.

8. Matthew 9:20–22.

9. John 12:1–7.

10. Lou Engle, *Nazirite DNA* (n.p.:, n.d.). Book available from International House of Prayer website store, http://store.ihop.org/store/ product/11439/Nazirite-DNA/, and TheCall website store, http://www.thecall .com/Publisher/Article.aspx?ID=1000105042.

Chapter 5—Snowflake in the Amazon

1. See Proverbs 3:5–6.

2. LivingWithJoyRadio.com, "Interview with Dr. James Dobson, part 1," aired April 26, 2010, http://www.livingwithjoyradio.com/ programs/2010/4/26/interview-james-dobson-part-1/ (accessed July 21, 2011).

3. Wikipedia.com, s.v. "Amazon River," http://en.wikipedia.org/wiki/ Amazon_River (accessed July 22, 2011).

4. See John 7:38.

Notes

Chapter 6—Hunger Meets Hunger

1. Esther 4:15–16.
2. Esther 7–8.
3. Luke 10:19.
4. Mark 2:19–20.
5. John 4:32–34.
6. Revelation 5:8.
7. Matthew 15:24.
8. See Ephesians 2:10.
9. Mark 5:30.

Chapter 7—You Can't Do God's Will With Human Zeal

1. Genesis 6; Matthew 24:37–39.
2. Galatians 5:17.
3. Matthew 26:53–54.
4. Leonard Ravenhill, *Why Revival Tarries* (Bloomington, MN: Bethany House Publishers, 1959, 1987), 39.
5. 1 Kings 21:23; 2 Kings 9:10, 30–37.
6. James 4:8.

Chapter 8—Flourishing in Troubled Times

1. Jim Swanson, "Palm Trees," *Evidence of Design* (blog), June 12, 2009, http://www.evidenceofdesign.com/palm-trees/ (accessed July 22, 2011).
2. Matthew 8:16–27.
3. Philippians 4:11–12.
4. Duncan Campbell, "Revival in the Hebrides (1949)," transcript of a message delivered by Duncan Campbell in 1968, http://www.enterhisrest.org/charismata/revival_connection.pdf (accessed July 22, 2011).
5. Bill Bright, "7 Basic Steps to Successful Fasting and Prayer," Campus Crusade for Christ International, http://www.ccci.org/training-and-growth/devotional-life/7-steps-to-fasting/index.htm (accessed July 22, 2011).

Chapter 9—The Main Dish

1. Genesis 19:3.
2. Isaiah 58:7.
3. Acts 16:20–34.
4. Matthew 6:11.

Chapter 10—Living Inside Out

1. See Romans 14:16.

2. Matthew 28:19.

3. Matthew 6:6, KJV.

4. Ephesians 1:13–14.

Chapter 11—Extreme Makeover

1. TLC.com, "What Not to Wear," http://tlc.howstuffworks.com/tv/what -not-to-wear (accessed July 25, 2011).

2. Luke 8:26–39.

3. Isaiah 61:3.

4. Luke 15:22.

5. Joshua 10:12–14.

6. Luke 11:5–9.

7. Luke 18:1–8.

8. Matthew 15:21–28.

9. Elmer Towns, *The Beginner's Guide to Fasting*, 2nd ed. (Ventura, CA: Regal Books, 2001, 2009), 7–8.

Chapter 12—The Quit Option

1. Matthew 26:53.

2. Colossians 3:2.

3. I do want to warn anyone interested in reading the book *Lone Survivor* that, while it gives an honest account of training and intense battle, it also contains a high level of rough language/profanity.

4. Marcus Luttrell, *Lone Survivor: The Eyewitness Account of Operation Redwing and the Lost Heroes of SEAL Team 10* (New York: Hachette Book Group, 2008), 63.

5. Ibid., 94.

6. Ibid., 160.

7. Ibid., 140–141.

8. Ibid., 156.

FREE NEWSLETTERS
TO HELP EMPOWER YOUR LIFE

Why subscribe today?

☐ **DELIVERED DIRECTLY TO YOU.** All you have to do is open your inbox and read.

☐ **EXCLUSIVE CONTENT.** We cover the news overlooked by the mainstream press.

☐ **STAY CURRENT.** Find the latest court rulings, revivals, and cultural trends.

☐ **UPDATE OTHERS.** Easy to forward to friends and family with the click of your mouse.

CHOOSE THE E-NEWSLETTER THAT INTERESTS YOU MOST:

- Christian news
- Daily devotionals
- Spiritual empowerment
- And much, much more

SIGN UP AT: **http://freenewsletters.charismamag.com**

8178